Celebrating Celibacy

*15 Answers to the Most Popular Questions
About Abstinence*

F.S. Mitchell

To my cousin
Justin,

You have grown up to be a very
handsome & respectable young man'
You will always be welcomed to stay with
us - I hope we can show you Germany
before we leave -
I pray that you will have a blessed year-
Thanks for your encouragement -

Much love,
Cousin Frances

Dedication

In Loving Memory of

Etzer Robert Pierre-Louis Jr.
Who lived his life for the Lord.

Thank you for inspiring so many people including myself
with your faith.
Your desire to serve the Lord in your waiting has become
my goal.
Your purpose was far greater than you imagined. Rest in
peace.

*"His Lord said to him,
'Well done, good and faithful servant;
you were faithful over a few things,
I will make you ruler over many things.
Enter into the joy of your Lord."
(Author's adaptation)
Matthew 25:21*

A
Special Thanks
to my mother
Liz

Thank you for teaching me how to live a life worth celebrating. It was you who told me that the Lord would bless me with a good husband if I waited to experience sex in marriage. Because of your teaching and your love for me, my blessing came to pass with my husband, Mitch.

Mitch
You are my husband, my lover, my friend and my TESTIMONY!
Thank you for all of your patience, support, and your faith. I could not have completed this assignment without you. You are my reward.

Special thanks!

Thank You, Lord, for the opportunity to write this testimony. The very fact that I can share this story shows triumph. Your Spirit kept me. You are the One who is responsible for my victory, and for that I say, "Thank You."

Lord, I never said I was perfect and on many of my dates, I certainly wasn't perfect. I did compromise, I did fall into temptation and I did put myself in risky situations. However, I remained celibate because You were there with me. You made my walk of celibacy possible. I couldn't have done it without You.

For all those times I sat on the edge of some boy's bed feeling convicted to tears and/or convicted enough to change my mind from going any further, I thank You.

Thank You for the time You kept me when a date served me a drink full of liquor without my knowledge. He knew I never drank before so he tried to trick me. His intentions were to make me drunk so that I wouldn't be on my guard. You, however, were on guard. The drink didn't work and the date was so curious he actually took a sip of the drink wondering why it had no effect on me. Later, after curiosity got the best of him, he told me of his intentions. I told him about Your intentions for me. With Your help, that weapon formed against me didn't prosper.

Thank You for the time I dated the 200+ pound football player from a nearby college. The school year was ending and I finally had a chance to go out with this handsome young man. After two dates, we became close friends and would spend hours talking about Your goodness. One night after a movie date, he invited me to his dorm room. He said he wanted to show me his bedroom and how cool he had decorated it. I thought it was strange for someone to invite me to see a dorm room packed away in boxes. The remaining students were to leave the next morning. I almost fell for it but seeing that it was an all-male dorm, I didn't want to risk the chance of getting into trouble for breaking the rules.

He would have had to sneak me in and I didn't want to do that. I'm so glad I was obedient to those simple dorm rules because there is no telling what would have happened to me in that dorm. With very few people left on campus and me being the only female, accompanying a 200+ pound man, I could have been attacked by my date as well as others on that floor. That was an accident ready to happen. I am grateful for the security guard who sent me on my way for being parked in the parking lot for so long.

Thank You for the time You protected me at that military party. The young man I met earlier that week was so charismatic. I thought it was romantic to have him invite me to his party. With my mother's permission, I decided to attend with a friend and call my mom as soon as I got there. My friend backed out of going so I went alone. Just before I approached the door, I saw a woman dressed in a short, white negligee and high heels. She had come out of the room where the party was held. The woman looked like a prostitute! She walked back into the room and the door was closed behind her. This was my first chance to leave the place but I think my curiosity got the best of me and I really wanted to see where my new friend was. A few minutes later, I knocked on the door to see my "date." Three men answered the door.

One said, "Hey, he is busy right now, um want me to get him?" Angrily, I said, "Yes, tell him I'm here." When my so-called date for the night came to the door, he was falling out of his clothes, tripping over his feet and could barely even speak to me. He smiled and thanked me for coming and quickly excused himself and went back inside. I left so fast fearful that he might come back out and ask me in. I never wanted to see him again. I am so thankful that You allowed me to see what was going on before I got inside that room. Bless You, Lord!

Thank You for forgiving me all the times I let my guard down and got my feelings and desires all stirred up. I let You down numerous times. I should have been wiser, should have been more careful and should have been obedient. So again I thank You for keeping me. You not only spoke to me when the temptation became great but You spoke to the other person as well.

Lord, I thank you for the people you put in my path who blessed me. Like the man who treated me more like a little sister than a girlfriend. He told me all about the secrets of men. He told me what men wanted, and he told me why men acted the way they did. Although he pursued me he never pressured me for sex. He explained that if I were to sleep with him it would not only hurt me physically because it was my first time but also hurt me emotionally because he wouldn't be committed to me afterwards.

Thank You for allowing him to be so honest with me. He taught me valuable lessons. He also knew how I wanted to wait until marriage and to please You. So, he would say that having sex with him prior to marriage would only cause me bitterness and regret. He told me that the experience would be hard for me to get over and that if I truly wanted to wait then I should wait to share that (virginity) with my husband because I could never take it back. Thank You, Lord, for sending that man my way to minister to me. I was at a weak point in my life, and he had to show me the way!

Weeks before my wedding day some of my trusted friends and family members told me that it was okay for me to have sex with my fiancé since he was my husband-to-be. Thank You for telling me not to give in. The wedding day would have been different. Our honeymoon would not have been the same either. I would have been sorry for not waiting. Thank You for speaking to my fiancé as well, for he gave me great encouragement in my weakest moments. He thought if I had sex with him prior to marriage after waiting for so long, that I would be angry with him afterwards and would regret that special moment. He too wanted us to wait. It was a challenge, but Lord, I do thank You for keeping us. He thanks You, too.

Contents

Preface

Celebrating Celibacy

The intent of this book is to answer the most popular questions that female teenagers and young adults have about abstinence. By no means does this book encourage women not to marry. Nor does this book attempt to promote negative views about sex.

Sex is a wonderful gift that God designed for us to experience in marriage; however, sex is easily perverted and portrayed in many negative ways especially in the media. The Lord is not pleased with acts of fornication.

I pray that this book will encourage single women to abstain from sexual relationships until marriage, develop an intimate relationship with the Lord and celebrate singleness!

To be single means to be separated from others or set apart. The American Heritage dictionary defines single as, "to choose or distinguish from others: *singled her out for praise.*"

Celebrate is defined as: "to perform (a ritual, etc.) publicly and formally solemnize, to proclaim; to honor or praise publicly 2. Perform a religious ceremony"

So I charge you to proclaim your new lifestyle of holiness and to honor and praise your Lord and Savior by living a lifestyle that is pleasing to Him.

Introduction

Celebrating Celibacy began over 20 years ago in seed form when my mother told me that waiting to experience sex in marriage would please God and produce a blessing— a "good husband." As a child and young teenager, my desires were to please my mom and dad as well as my Heavenly Father. I decided to wait. My desires were to be a "good girl" and receive a blessing— a "good husband." Until that time, I didn't know many "good husbands." Most of the husbands I heard about were alcoholics, wife beaters, and cheaters. I wanted to have a good one.

As a teenager, I began dating. The journey of celibacy created many frustrations. With dating came rejection, peer pressure, isolation, and eventually, low self-esteem. My faith, however, never wavered. I still wanted to wait.

While in college, I saw so many horrible things. My friends were experiencing sex, yet suffering emotionally, physically, and spiritually. Some contracted diseases. Many became pregnant. A few became emotionally damaged and eventually left the university. When I realized how premarital sex damages young women in every area of their lives, I decided to talk openly about my lifestyle of celibacy in the hopes of helping young women and teens.

I found a teaching ministry with my home church, Sanctuary of God. Young people became my spiritual challenge. As I grew closer to the Lord in Spirit, my faith grew. With time, I began to do some teaching and ministering of my own. Teaching teenage girls, telling them that they were special, warning them about the potential dangers of premarital sex, and encouraging them to wait, gave me great joy. I used the questions polled from the teens and young women in seminars and workshops and made them into chapter titles.

PART I

What Is So Good About Abstaining From Sex?

CHAPTER 1

Question One: Why Wait?

Celebrating Celibacy!

Why Celebrate Celibacy?

In Any town, USA, there are countless females making life-changing decisions. At this moment, a teenaged girl is waiting for a pregnancy test to display one pink line or two. She paces the floor desperately trying to think of a plan of action for each result. Meanwhile a college freshman is contemplating spending her spring semester book money to end her pregnancy. Elsewhere a single woman who recently started dating the "man of her dreams" cries in shame trying to figure out why she has been experiencing discomfort down there. She feels betrayed, neglected, and heartbroken. She can't believe that her new relationship produced such physical and emotional pain.

Even as you read the pages of this book, another young woman, perhaps your neighbor's daughter or your co-worker's sister, sits in a clinic waiting for lab results. She is praying that it's nothing. She believes that she is pregnant. Then she considers the possibility of an STD. Finally she decides that she should have waited.

With scenarios such as these, it is no wonder why more and more females are deciding on abstinence. Celibacy has become the solution for many because of damaging sexual relationships, soul-ties, and religious beliefs. Some women simply want to find themselves again and/or empower themselves.

The best way I can describe celibacy is abstaining or refraining from sexual activities until you are married. I chose celibacy as a lifestyle because I wanted to wait to experience sex with my husband. Choosing celibacy allowed me the opportunity to worship the Lord in my "waiting." Saving yourself for marriage is a cause for celebration!

Celebrating celibacy also stands for celebrating your singleness. As a single woman, abstinence is important because each time you have sex with another, you marry in spirit. Apostle Paul writes:

I Corinthians 6:15-17
Do you not know that your bodies are members of Christ?
Shall I then take the members of Christ and make them
members of a harlot? Certainly not!
Or do you not know that he who is joined to a harlot
is one body with her?
For "the two," He says, "shall become one flesh."
But he who is joined to the Lord is one spirit with Him.

This scripture encourages us to flee from sexual activities because each time we participate in sexual activities we sin against our own bodies. Abstaining from sexual activities prior to marriage keeps you from being spiritually tied to another. This gives you freedom.

Another way to describe celibacy is to glorify God with your bodies.

I Corinthians 6:19-20
Or do you not know that your body is the temple of the
Holy Spirit who is in you, whom you have from God, and
you are not your own?
For you were bought at a price; therefore glorify God in
your body and in your spirit, which are God's.

When Jesus died, He paid the price for our bodies as well as our souls. His death birthed our freedom. In celibacy you are free to worship and honor the Lord in your waiting and become one with the Lord. This alone is cause for celebration.

Celebrating can also be described as performing a religious ceremony and/or honoring or praising publicly. Celebrating can also be defined as worship. Worship is how we show reverence to God.

In celibacy, you worship and praise the Lord with your waiting. Your devotion to the Lord is a good thing. You should be happy with your service to Him. Enjoy each moment and reflect on His goodness.

We know what it means to celebrate, so what is celibacy exactly?

The American Heritage Dictionary defines celibate as: "Abstaining from sexual intercourse, esp. by reason of religious vows. 2. Unmarried."

To abstain is defined as: "to refrain from something by one's own choice. 2. Abstinence means to deliberately self-restrain. b. Abstention from sexual activity; continence."

This is what celibacy is all about, self-restraint and self-control! You have the power to choose. (*Galatians 5:22-23*).

My Cause for Celebration!

At the age of 22, I was dating a respectable young man I'll call "Raymond." For months there was no intimate contact between us. However, I was beginning to feel pressure from him. Even though my desires were to wait and experience sex only in marriage, I was battling with trying to please the man with whom I had fallen in love as well as trying to please God.

Raymond was experienced sexually and wanted nothing more than to have sex with me. We didn't share the same spiritual beliefs therefore I constantly struggled throughout the relationship. Because temptation played such a major role with my emotions, I began making bad decisions. I began to experiment with him. He taught me all sorts of things. Eventually, kissing turned into necking. Necking turned into touching. Touching turned into fondling and playing with each other. This level of intimacy wasn't enough for him, however. He wanted sex, and he reminded me of this each time we were together. Temptation along with his pressure eventually won me over to the point that I actually considered having sex with him. One night I decided to become "experienced," and I told him I wanted to try sex for the first time.

After waiting for so many years, I was about to experience sex and I was about to learn everything about life, or so I thought. No longer would I be left out of conversations. Even as a teenager and young adult, I firmly protested against premarital sex but now, I thought I would be able to relate to my friends who bragged about their sexual experiences.

How exciting, how thrilling, how foolish! I found myself saying "I want to do this," and then questioning myself, "Am I really going to do this?"

There I was sitting on the edge of Raymond's bed kissing him. Whenever Raymond touched me, I felt butterflies in my stomach. Raymond touched my body and it felt wonderful but I kept thinking, "Am I really doing this?" I was so excited yet nervous at the same time. All types of thoughts were in my mind. I thought, "Does Ray love me?" while allowing him to undress me. Then I thought, "I wonder if he will be gentle with me or is this experience all about him?" He took off his shirt, then mine. He undid his pants, then mine. The situation was no longer romantic. It wasn't like a normal night of playful exploration. This night was different. Raymond was more forceful, determined, and serious. All of a sudden, I felt trapped. I couldn't breathe. My air became tight. I felt like I was being softly pressed forward toward a cliff. I felt my muscles bracing to resist the fall.

When Raymond leaned in to kiss me, a rush of emotions came over me. I was so overwhelmed that I burst into tears, tears of protest. I just couldn't do it. My answer was, "No, I just can't do this!" It still is. Better yet the answer is, "I am waiting for marriage and until then, I am celebrating celibacy."

Thinking back on that night when I almost gave in, I am so thankful for that tearful outburst. Mentally, I thought I was ready, and physically, I felt ready. Emotionally, I was not. I remember crying to that young man and saying, "I am sorry, I can't, I just can't."

The Lord knew my concerns, heard my prayers and provided an escape for me. That escape was an overwhelming release of emotions and stress. I couldn't help but cry. Time spent in that relationship made me feel obligated to please Raymond. I didn't like to feel rushed or pressured and I just couldn't handle my internal struggles. The stress stemmed from the dilemma of giving away something that I wanted to keep. I was trying so hard to keep a relationship thriving by giving up something that would upset me.

The relationship ended shortly after that night. Raymond was considerate of my feelings and he understood my wishes. The Lord touched his heart and kept us both. Our "first time" was simply not meant to be and neither was our future together.

I remember driving out to the beach the next day. The day was absolutely beautiful. The breeze from the ocean cooled my skin while the rays of the sun warmed it. I could taste the ocean through the breeze. I noticed everything that day. Beautiful stones and shells produced patterns in the sand. The sand felt warm under my feet. I remember feeling like a little girl wearing my blue and white bathing suit, hair pulled back in a bun, and hopping and skipping without a care in the world. I felt so free. There were no feelings of guilt. I was happy and cheerful, with no worries whatsoever. There were no thoughts of "what if I am pregnant" nor "what have I done" nor "what if Raymond doesn't love me" or "what if he leaves me now?" Instead, my thoughts were "Yes!" I did not cave in. I am still a virgin. I am still the same.

Thinking back to that summer I remember feeling young, inexperienced and a little confused. Regardless of the confusion, I was well aware that I had so much to celebrate. I celebrated not having my name dragged through the gutter by Raymond. I celebrated my will power. I celebrated not being another girl on the list of girls Raymond slept with. I celebrated God's deliverance and guidance. I celebrated not having to hang my head down in shame in front of Raymond's friends. I celebrated freedom. I celebrated CELIBACY!

Celibacy is a lifestyle for me. It's one that I have grown to love and one that I am very proud of. I enjoy this guilt/worry/pressure free lifestyle. I have so many things to look forward to. Why not wait and experience something so sacred and pure with that special man, my future husband?

Life is too short to be depressed, boggled down with unnecessary fears, hurts or desires that stem from unhealthy sexual relationships. I have many responsibilities, but nothing like running out for baby formula or diapers or to the nearby pharmacy for protection like pills or condoms. I am drug free. There are no chemicals in my system to prevent childbirth. No tragic/immoral decisions that would prevent childbirth.

Abstinence is a method of birth control that is guaranteed to work. Abstaining gives you freedom. You have the opportunity to live a life that is full of choices. You can choose freedom and freedom births life. Jesus said:

"I have come that they may have life, and that they may have it more abundantly" John 10:10

Having a spiritual connection with Jesus allows you such freedom. I see abstaining as a method of obtaining total freedom. You may feel restricted and limited, but you access so much freedom when you decide to wait. You will be free from soul–ties or spiritual connections with other men.

Galatians 5:1
Stand fast therefore in the liberty (freedom) by which Christ has made us free, and do not be entangled again with a yoke of bondage.

Liberty means freedom. And where the Spirit of the Lord is, there is freedom. *II Corinthians 3:17*

What do you have to lose? Even if you have been sexually active in the past, you can ask the Lord to deliver you from any soul-ties you may have created. Ask the Lord to remove you out from any sexually premature relationships. Desire your freedom and the Lord will bless you. Living a lifestyle of celibacy is definitely a process. You can't do it without the Spirit of the Lord. It is the Holy Spirit that brings us to forgiveness, holiness, sanctification, and service to God.

Ezekiel 36:27
"I will put My Spirit within you and cause you to walk in
My statues, and you will keep My judgments and do them."

I believe that abstaining is easier when you do not know what you are missing. So, in other words, don't start fondling or allowing someone to fondle you. Don't experiment with giving one another pleasure because your emotions and desires will become stirred up. It will become harder to stop yourself from going all the way. Just don't start! There is no rush to explore that lifestyle. Desire yourself in the Lord and continue to *celebrate celibacy*!

Prayer

I Thessalonians 5:23
"Now may the God of peace Himself sanctify
you completely;
and may your whole spirit, soul, and body be preserved
blameless at the coming of our Lord Jesus Christ."

I now charge you by the Lord to be epistles well read
to all brethren.

I Thessalonians 5:27
(Author's interpretation of scripture)

May the grace of our Lord Jesus Christ be with you.
Amen

CHAPTER 2

Question 2:
What If He Says He Loves Me?

AGAPE vs. EROS

I Corinthians 13:4-8

Love suffers long and is kind;
love does not envy;
love does not parade itself, is not puffed up;
Does not behave rudely,
does not seek its own, is not provoked, thinks no evil;
does not rejoice in iniquity, but rejoices in the truth;
Bears all things, believes all things, hopes all things,
endures all things,
Love never fails.

What if he says he loves me? Believe it or not, this question is the second most popular question asked by teenagers and adults in seminars and workshops. My friend *Dana married right out of high school and divorced soon after. After entering the dating game again, she found celibacy difficult. She called me late one night frantic. Her new boyfriend began to put pressure on her. He had given her an ultimatum telling her that he wanted to see other people because he wanted more intimacy in their relationship.

Dana said, "He said that 'we should have sex by now, girl.' "What if he really does love me?"

I couldn't believe my ears. Dana had just started dating this guy. She was completely torn by her decision to wait and with pleasing her new boyfriend. "I'm missing out girl, she said, sitting here playing Miss Goodie Two-Shoes when I really want to be with him.' 'Fran, deep down I want to do the right thing but I don't want this relationship to end. He could be my future husband!"

A few things were wrong with Dana's observation. First, she was totally uncomfortable with the pressure. The constant pressure sent her into a frenzy. If anyone makes you feel this unstable and desperate to please them, it's not a good thing. Second, the relationship was only a few weeks old. Dana told her boyfriend about her decisions to abstain. However, due to the two of them acting on their physical urges early on, the boyfriend applied additional pressure on her. Third, Dana commented that she wanted to save their relationship because he could be her future husband. If the boyfriend really wanted to marry Dana, why would he have given her an ultimatum?

It's so easy to be on the outside looking in, however, when you are going through the motions of a romantic relationship, and it's hard to see the big picture. Our one true reality is that everyone wants to be loved. Love is motivating, powerful, and liberating. It's essential to recognize what type of love motivates you. What type of love is necessary in your life? Is it romantic, physical, and conditional love? Perhaps you need another type of love that is unconditional, pure, and never ending.

This chapter takes a look at two loves. This breakdown is to help you discover which love is temporary and which love lasts forever.

Love Temporary

At the age of five, I fell in love. I fell in love with another kindergartner in my class. He had thick black hair, big brown eyes, and a toothless grin. His name was Jack and I loved him. For five, Jack was a dreamy little boy. I remember feeling so special when he held my hand underneath the table while the librarian read stories to the class. This was our special routine. I also recall how we wanted to sleep next to each other during naptime. He would pull his mat next to mine. We were in love.

Love, however, ended when we received a report card stating, "PROMOTED TO THE FIRST GRADE." We no longer shared our naptime, snack time, or library time. We were in different classes, with new teachers, new friends, and perhaps pursuing new loves.

Relationships today don't differ too much from those we had in our younger years. All relationships start the same. Attraction draws us in and we act from there. That temporary love or romantic love is called Eros.

EROS:

Eros is described as romantic or physical love. Eros can also be referred to as lusting, or love for passion. This love is conditional, meaning that it's temporary. This love has the potential to change quickly and end quickly. It simply doesn't last.

With Eros, there are many doubts. There are no guarantees in an Eros/romantic relationship. An Eros relationship could produce thoughts of why me, why now, how did I get pregnant, how did I contract this STD, my body is filthy, dirty, defiled, damaged, and used. Eros relationships tend to be followed by states of depression and loneliness.

Once the relationship, the romance and the passion fail, some crave to be back in the midst of it again. We long to be held again. We miss the closeness of this counterfeit love relationship and the false sense of sincerity and security. The relationship was a temporal pleasure and the only thing we are left with is an empty feeling.

Some believe that sex is love. Please know that this is far from the truth. Have you watched any talk shows lately where young girls are bragging about how many men they have slept with? So many times, young girls equate sex with love. They actually believe that having numerous partners is something to brag about! These girls are led to believe that the men who are sleeping with them must care about them, want to be with them and love them. However, those men seek to fulfill their own desires and afterwards leave these young girls alone. It's a sad and sick cycle, and I see it everyday on college campuses and in schools.

Such temporal relationships leave women feeling abused, lonely, depressed, and neglected, with low self-esteem and without self-worth. It's an everyday reality that needs to be stopped. Sisters in Christ, if you want to be loved, go to the Father! He can heal you and restore you to your proper place. He can provide everlasting, unconditional, agape love. He only desires your obedience, your praise, and your love!

Love Everlasting

God is Love and He never fails. Love is a necessity. We can't function without love. Do you know how much Jesus loves you? I do! One Sunday I recognized the power of Christ's love for me while sitting in a service listening to a pastor speak. The pastor began to describe how Jesus was dying on the cross and how He cried out in pain. The visual that I imagined was powerful. I became upset and overjoyed simultaneously at the thought of Jesus suffering for my sake. Jesus suffered so that I might live.

I began to cry because at that moment I was feeling so much love that it overwhelmed me. Right where I was sitting, in the middle of the pew amongst 30 other people, I was experiencing the love that the Lord had for me. I cried because I was happy. I cried because I realized what a great sacrifice was made for me. I cried for that perfect, most precious act of love that set me free. Jesus suffered and died so that I might live. I was overwhelmed with love.

AGAPE:

Agape is God's perfect love; love unconditional. Unconditional love is faultless and never changing. It gets better and better. We delight ourselves in His perfect love. This is the type of love that keeps us and motivates us. We can trust this type of love. Experiencing this love sets you free, free from the bondage of doubt, worries, fears, negative consequences, and insecurities. Agape love is perfect. Why not embrace this kind of love and celebrate it?

The Samaritan woman

Do you remember the Samaritan women who went to draw water from the well? She did not know Jesus but after a brief encounter with Him, she knew Him. She experienced Love.

John 4:7
A woman of Samaria came to draw water:
Jesus said to her, "Give Me a drink."

Jesus asked this woman for a drink. Not knowing who Jesus was, she asked why she should give Him to drink for He was a Jew. Jesus went on to teach her in a loving manner despite her ignorance. Jesus answered and said to her, "*If you knew the gift of God, and who it is who says to you, 'Give Me a drink,' you would have asked Him, and He would have given you living water.*" John 4:10

Jesus began to love this woman to Salvation. He explained in *John 4:13-14*, "*Whoever drinks of this water will thirst again,* (well water) *but whoever drinks of the water that I shall give him will never thirst. But the water that I shall give him will become in him a fountain of water springing up into everlasting life.*"

Jesus then began to tell her about her very own life. The woman then believed that He was a prophet and so she questioned His places of worship. The Lord educated her regarding true worship. *John 4:23-24*, "*But the hour is coming, and now is when the true worshipers will worship the Father in spirit and truth; for the Father is seeking such to worship Him. God is Spirit and those who worship Him must worship in spirit and truth.*"

This was good information for her because at this time Samaritans did not know how to worship and many were confused regarding the subject. Do you recognize how gentle the Lord was with this woman? In the short time He spent with the Samaritan woman, the townspeople started talking amongst themselves asking why Jesus would talk to such a woman. The townspeople were actually wondering if Jesus knew whom He was dealing with. Of course He knew. He is all knowing.

Jesus knew that the woman was a sinner. The Lord knew she had been with five husbands and was living with a man who was not her husband. Don't you know that Jesus knows exactly where you are? Don't you know that He loves you and that He desires good things for you? As for the Samaritan woman, Jesus desired for her to be educated, corrected, and saved. Therefore He taught her about the things of God, the proper way of worship, and introduced and offered Himself, Salvation.

The Samaritan woman accepted Jesus and ran back to tell the town of Samaria about a man she met. She was loved by Jesus and then led many others to Him through her salvation. The Lord loved the Samaritan woman unconditionally despite her sin.

That day at the well she met Real Love!

Let's compare and contrast:

AGAPE	EROS
unconditional	conditional
free	expensive
beneficial	selfish benefits
grace	self seeking
unlimited	restricted, ties, bonds
righteous, holy	sinful
uncalculated	manipulative,
no rejection	rejection
love that builds	love that tears apart
love that heals	destructive
guaranteed	no guarantee
trusted	not trustworthy
peaceful	chaotic
pure	lustful
patient	pressure, forceful
kind	merciless
humble	arrogant
no compromise	compromises
everlasting	fleeting

These descriptions of love demonstrate what type of love is necessary and what love is everlasting. Agape love is beneficial in so many ways. All of your needs, hopes, dreams, desires, and comfort, are possible with Agape love. Agape love will keep you in perfect peace.

We should continue to focus on the love of God and pray that we do not become too distracted by Eros (romantic/physical love). Do all you can to please the Lord. Remember you don't have to please man nor do you have to do anything to be loved. You are already loved <u>perfectly</u>.

The need to be loved by someone is human nature. However, we need to first recognize what type of love is the most important to us, the most valuable. The Lord wants you to be satisfied and fulfilled with His love. The Lord desires that you give yourself to Him completely. He desires that you put Him first in your life. He desires intimacy!

Intimacy

An intimate relationship is a very personal one. The American Heritage Dictionary defines the word intimate as essential and innermost. Intimacy is also defined as "familiarity or close acquaintance." It's essential to have an intimate relationship with the Lord. Once you form an intimate relationship, your life will become more meaningful. You will become complete!

When we form intimate relationships with men, we long to spend all of our time with them and we desperately want to trust them. In singleness, spend your time with Jesus. Learn to trust, obey, and study the Word. Once you have established a stronger friendship with Jesus, you can then easily put past relationships, the present pursuers, yearning after what other people have, and your own willful ways aside. You will be able to see the Lord's sovereign plan for your life.

Jeremiah: 29:11
For I know the thoughts I think toward you, says the Lord,
thoughts of peace and not of evil, to give you
a future and a hope.

Wait on the blessing of the Lord and expect great things. Don't worry about being single or not ever having someone to *love* you. You are already loved perfectly. You may be single now but be of good cheer. Perhaps the Lord is preparing a mate for you right now. When the Lord completes preparing you and your future mate, He will bring the two of you together. Once you meet the man that the Lord selected, you will be so delighted with him because the Lord will continue to love you through that mate. It's all by design, so never worry or get anxious looking for someone (*Philippians 4:6*). The Lord desires a love relationship with you. He wants you to be content with Him. He is always able to supply all of your needs.

Recognize that Jesus is the Word and in the Word you will find numerous love letters from the Lord to His people. The Word is filled with many promises, encouraging words, and truths to give you hope.

These love scriptures are a small sample of what the Word provides. The more you read and study the Word, the more intimate you become with the Father.

Love scriptures:

Genesis 22:14
"Jehovah jireh" The Lord provides!
He is a Provider! He will provide all of your needs.

Psalm 23:1
"The Lord is my shepherd; I shall not want"

The Lord is your Protector. He knows exactly where you are at all times. You can never leave His sight. He watches over you and protects you like a Good Shepherd. He is so good to you. He takes care of all of your needs.
You shall not want for anything!

I John 3: 1-5
Behold what manner of love the Father has bestowed on us,
that we should be called children of God!

We are without a doubt King's kids! Why not think of the Lord as your Daddy!
Refer to Him as your Dad, "Abba," for He is your Heavenly Father.

I John 3:3
And everyone who has this hope in Him purifies himself,
just as He is pure.

All who believe in Him and have His spirit are born-again in the family of God.
We are His children!

Ephesians 1: 13-14 (Sealed)
In Him you also trusted, after you heard the word of truth,
the gospel of your salvation;
in whom also, having believed, you were sealed with the
Holy Spirit of promise,
who is the guarantee of our inheritance until
the redemption of the purchased possession,
to the praise of His glory.

Sisters, you are the chosen ones.
You were not picked over or left out.
You were chosen!

Ephesians 1 3:5 (Chosen Ones)
Blessed be the God and Father of our Lord Jesus Christ,
who has blessed us with every spiritual
blessing in heavenly places in Christ,
just as He chose us in Him before the foundation
of the world,
that we should be holy and without blame
before Him in love,
having predestined us to adoption as sons
by Jesus Christ to Himself,
according to the good pleasure of His will,
to the praise of the glory of His grace
by which He made us accepted in the Beloved.

Do you know what it feels like to be chosen? Perhaps you can relate to what it feels like to be the last one selected or picked for a game or activity. If so, then you may have also questioned your very own worth. But you don't have to question your worth with God. You are worth more than the price of rubies to Him

Proverbs 31:10
Who can find a virtuous wife? For her worth is far above
rubies.

The Lord sends us Help, His Spirit!

Romans 5:5
Now hope does not disappoint, because the love of God has
been poured out in our hearts by the Holy Spirit who was
given to us.

The relationship you have with the Lord should be
an intimate one.

It is a relationship comprised of you, the Father, the Son,
and the Holy Spirit.
Stay connected!

John 17:23
"I in them, and You in Me;
that they may be made perfect in one,
and that the world may know that You have sent Me,
and have loved them as you have loved Me."

You can find contentment in Christ. He is always there with
you by your side!

Hebrews 13:5
Let your conduct be without covetousness; be content with
such things as you have. For He Himself has said,
"I will never leave you nor forsake you."

People may change but the Lord stays the same.
Jesus is the same always.

Hebrews 13:8
Jesus Christ is the same yesterday, today, and forever.

The Lord is an awesome friend. He knows exactly
how to comfort you!
He doesn't want you to worry for He is concerned
about your future.
He is looking out for you!

John 14:1-9
Let not your heart be troubled; you believe in God,
believe also in Me.
"In My Father's house are many mansions;
if it were not so, I would have told you,

I go to prepare a place for you."

The Lord will not allow anything to separate the love
He has for you.
He will love you always.

Romans 8:38-39
For I am persuaded that neither death nor life,
nor angels
nor principalities
nor powers,
nor things present
nor things to come,
nor height
nor depth,
nor any other created thing,
shall be able to separate us from
the love of God
which is in
Christ Jesus our Lord.

Write your own scriptural love letter and learn how much
the Lord loves you!
Read your love letter daily and be content, be encouraged,
and be loved perfectly.

Prayer

Lord, I thank You for Your perfect love,
Your perfect and unchanging ways.
I thank You for always being there and never
leaving me nor forsaking me.
Thank You for forgiving me when I sinned against You.

Please keep me, Lord, so that I may please You
and that I may delight in You and so You can delight in me.

Lord, Teach me Your ways.
In my walk of celibacy help me to recognize
which love is essential.

Help me to recognize how much You love me so I
can let go of poor relationships.
Help me to be intimate with You, Lord.
Give me a spirit of thankfulness
so that I may learn to appreciate Your perfect love.

CHAPTER 3

Question 3:
He Thinks I'm the Most Beautiful Woman He Has Ever Met, How Can I Leave Him?

YOU ARE BEAUTIFUL

Celebrating the beauty inside of you

A few years ago I met a young college student who was in trouble. This young lady, I'll call *Tammy, was facing the University Judicial Affairs Committee. Tammy asked me for prayer. When I asked her what she needed prayer for, she began to tell me how her life had begun a downward spiral. She was being accused of drug possession, assault, and several other campus violations.

Tammy said,

"I met the man of my dreams, *Jason. When I was broke, he paid my bills. When I needed books, he would buy them for me. He moved me in with him and we shared all of the bills, but things got bad after a month. He would come home late and would fight with me. I tried to leave him but he would beg me to stay. I know Jay loves me. He really does love me. After a while, he started selling drugs, but not the hard stuff. He taught me how to smoke. I didn't want to but he said that smoking made me sexy. A few of his boys stayed over one night after a party. He wanted me to sleep with them. I did. The next day he got angry with me and he kicked me out of the apartment. Right now, I'm homeless. I stay with one of the guys from the party. I don't like being at his place but I have no other place to go. Jason may take me back when he calms down. I have to prove to him that I love him. I know he loves me."

I then asked Tammy, "Don't you see, you can't go back to that lifestyle. Why not go home to your family for a while?"

Tammy said,

"He (Jason) thinks I'm the most beautiful woman
he has ever met.
Why would I ever leave him?"

This chapter was written for all the "Tammys" out there. It took me weeks to get over Tammy's decision to return to Jay. I couldn't convince this young woman to turn her life around. I prayed for her and left her with scripture. I have prayed everyday since I met her. A friend told me that I had to release Tammy and believe that God was going to bless her. God placed me in Tammy's path that day and I pray that the prayers and scriptures will be enough to change her path of destruction. I never saw Tammy again after that day but I think of her often.

Tammy's declaration of "He thinks I'm the most beautiful woman he has ever met," is a popular one with women. Why do so many of us hang on to every word from a man? Do you know who you really are? You are already beautiful. Allow this scripture to feed your spirit and give you a clear depiction of who you are to Jesus!

David said:

Psalms 139

"O Lord, You have searched me and known me.
You know my sitting down and my rising up;
You understand my thought afar off.
You comprehend my path and my lying down, and are
acquainted with all my ways. For there is not a word on my
tongue, but, behold, O Lord, You know it altogether.

You have hedged me behind and before,
and laid Your hand upon me.
Such knowledge is too wonderful for me; it is high,
I cannot attain it.

Where can I go from Your Spirit? Or where can I flee from
Your presence?

If I ascend into heaven, You art there;
If I make my bed in hell, behold, You are there
If I take the wings of the morning
And dwell in the uttermost parts of the sea,
Even there Your hand shall lead me,
And Your right hand shall hold me,
If I say, "Surely the darkness shall fall on me,"
Indeed, the darkness shall not hide from You,

But the night shines as the day;
The darkness and the light are both alike to You.

For You formed my inward parts;
You covered me in my mother's womb.
I will praise You, for I am fearfully and wonderfully made;
Marvelous are Your works,
And that my soul knows very well.
My frame was not hidden from You,
When I was made in secret,
And skillfully wrought in the lowest parts of the earth.
Your eyes saw my substance, being yet unformed.
And in Your book they all were,
The days fashioned for me,
When as yet there was none of them.

How precious also are Your thoughts to me, O God!
How great is the sum of them!
If I should count them, they would be more in number than
the sand;

When I awake, I am still with You.
Oh, that You would slay the wicked, O God!
Depart from me, therefore, you bloodthirsty men.
For they speak against You wickedly;
Your enemies take Your name in vain.
Do not I hate them, O Lord, who hate You?
And do I not loathe those who rise up against You?
I hate them with perfect hatred; I count them my enemies.

Search me, O God, and know my heart;
Try me, and know my anxieties;
And see if there is any wicked way in me,
And lead me in the way everlasting."

This scripture speaks to our lives, our self worth, and our self-esteem. In order for you to be successful celebrating celibacy you have to know who you are in Christ. You are beautiful to Him. This scripture also shows us that the Lord is concerned about every area of our lives. He knows our thoughts and even the words on our tongues. Trust me ladies, when God created us, He made no mistakes.

SELF IMAGE

A negative self-image can start as early as childhood. As a child, I had a different perception of myself than the rest of the world. Out of the other two siblings of mine, I knew that I was the "dark" one. One brother was brown and the other was light brown. I however, was "black." Everything about me was black or so I thought. I never questioned my race or gender. I was without a doubt a "black girl."

So, as a child I created drawings representing who I thought I was. I always drew smiling, happy faces with a skinny body and long hair (braids). One particular day in school, I colored in my skin a light brown color simply because the brown was being used by another student. The principal of the school came into the class and noticed my picture. He took a seat right beside me in one of those teeny tiny kindergartner chairs and spoke to me eye to eye.

After evaluating the photo he asked, "What color are you?"

I answered him, "Black."

Then he asked, what color is your hair?"

I answered, "Black."

His last question was, "What color are your eyes?"

I actually answered, "Black."

The principal then corrected me saying, " No my dear, see your skin, while pointing to my arm, " You are brown." 'And as for your eyes, they are brown, too.'

"They are?" I asked shocked.

"Yes they are dark brown, he said. 'And your hair is not black, it's brown, reddish brown." 'So when someone asks you, you say my eyes are brown, my skin is brown and my hair is brown.'

Mr. Quarles, my principal, showed me ME! Little ole' brown me. Up until that very moment, no one, not even my parents told me differently. What have your parents told you about yourself? Did they ever tell you how beautiful you are? Have they ever told you that you favor your grandmother or that you have your father's eyes? Who helped to shape your opinion of yourself? Was it a loved one or an enemy who wanted to hurt you? This is an important question because depending on who showed you, "you," you might be living a lie due to their opinion. You quite possibly haven't let go of those images from the past. Those painful moments, name-callings and insults could still affect your present day feelings about yourself. Again, I ask you, how did you form opinions of yourself?

The Word of God says that we are *"fearfully and wonderfully made."* We are here for a specific purpose. God is concerned about every part of our lives. God knew you before your were even born. *"Your eyes saw my substance, being yet unformed."*

The Lord desires for us to know that we are beautiful and special in His sight. He thinks about us. We are always on His mind. He even knows how many hairs are on our heads. *"How precious also are your thoughts to me, O God! How great is the sum of them."* This is why it's so important to know who you are in the Lord. *His thoughts of us out number the grains of sand.* Do you now see just how special you are to Him?

When we have discovered our place in Christ, it is much easier to do what the Lord has created us to do. This is how celibacy became easy for me because the more I stayed in the Word of God, the better I felt about my destination and myself. Live your life on purpose! Do what is right and acceptable according to the Word.

James 1:22, 25
Be doers of the word, and not hearers only, deceiving
yourselves.
But he who looks into the perfect law of liberty
and continues in it,
and is not a forgetful hearer but a doer of the work,
this one will be blessed in what he does.

Discovering the True Princess That You Are
You are a King's kid, a Princess!

As followers of Christ, we are King's kids! Now as a king's kids, we must remember our "royal" position, duties and behavior. Just because we are considered royalty, doesn't mean we can do whatever we like. We must obey the King, who is Christ Jesus and do what His Word has instructed.

Allow the title as "Princess" to fit your character. Your position or place in this world is to let the world see the goodness, love and light that shines in you, which is Christ Jesus. This light makes you beautiful.

Matthew 5:16
Let your light so shine before men, that they may see your
good works to glorify your Father in heaven.

We should be in a proper place in Him to serve and worship Him. We show the love of Christ by being witnesses for Jesus, and spreading the gospel through our very walk and talk. As princesses, we are to respect, honor, and obey the King. Let's imagine that the Lord "the King" called for you. Would you go? Would you be prepared and willing to submit to God's will?

Willingness is essential when you want to serve the King. Therefore, be prepared and be ready at all times. Act accordingly! Your role as princess does not give you permission to act foolishly! You are a person of noble character. You should also have the Spirit of God. You are to be wise, prepared, kind, generous, dutiful and obedient.

Wouldn't you like to be thought of as a virtuous woman? If so, you can't act unseemly. Everything about you including your clothing must say respect and dignity. Put on a royal attitude that honors the King.

Now that you know you are beautiful, well formed, well blessed, and much thought of, wouldn't you hate to lose your royal position? Losing your position is equivalent to losing your blessings. The Bible tells us of someone who actually lost her blessing out of disobedience to the King. She was a beautiful queen named Vashti.

Esther 1:10
The King asked his eunuchs to bring Queen Vashti
before him
wearing her royal crown, in order to show
her beauty to the people and the officials,
for
she was beautiful to behold.

When King Ahasuerus desired to see his wife the queen, she refused! Queen Vashti was unwilling. This was during a time period when people could lose their life for disobeying the King. Not enough information is offered as to why Queen Vashti disobeyed her husband. Perhaps she was angry, or perhaps she was busy. Regardless Queen Vashti rebelliousness displeased the King very much.

Esther 1:12
" ... *Queen Vashti refused to come at the King's command*
brought by his eunuchs; therefore the King was furious, and
his anger burned within him. "

Queen Vashti displeased the King and his men so much,
that they feared that her rebellious, disobedient character
would greatly influence the other wives. The servants didn't
want the other wives to behave in this manner, dishonoring
their husbands. They came up with a punishment for Queen
Vashti. The plan was to have Queen Vashti removed. They
wanted to make an example of her. She was to never be
called on again.

Esther 2:1-4
... *When the wrath of King Ahasuerus subsided,*
he remembered Vashti,
what she had done, and what had been decreed against her.
Then the king's servants who attended him said:

"Let beautiful young virgins be sought for the king; and let
the king appoint officers in all the provinces of his kingdom,
that they may gather all the beautiful young virgins to
Shushan the citadel, into the women's quarters....
.... And let beauty preparations be given them.
Then let the young woman who pleases the king be queen
instead of Vashti."
This thing pleased the king, and he did so.

A young Jewish girl named Esther was one of the young
virgins gathered up. Immediately she found favor with the
custodian of the women. She was given more beauty preparations than the others. She eventually was moved to the
best place in the house of the women with her very own
maidservants.

53

For an entire year the servants prepared her so that she might be suitable for the king. They perfumed her with oils and with fragrances. Esther was also taught how to act in the king's presence.

Esther 2: 17
"The king loved Esther more than all the other women,
and she obtained grace and favor in his sight more
than all the virgins;
so he set the royal crown upon her head
and
made her queen instead of Vashti."

God had a divine purpose for this young woman, Esther. She probably never imagined becoming a queen and/or even being a hero for her own people. Esther had an excellent character. She was brave, confident, obedient and willing. She trusted God.

Esther had a cousin named Mordecai who normally sat at the king's gates. One day Mordecai learned of a plot to eliminate the Jewish people. Mordecai informed Esther and asked her to make an appeal to the King to save the Jews. At this time, no one knew that Esther was a Jew. Esther ultimately put her own life on the line with the King by making her request known to save her people. Esther sent a message to Mordecai:

Esther 4:11
"….All the king's servants and the people of the king's
provinces know that any man or woman who goes into the
inner court to the king,
who has not been called, he has but one law:
put all to death,
except the one to whom the king holds out the golden
scepter, that he may live.

Yet I myself have not been called to go in to the king these thirty days."

Mordecai sent words back to Esther saying:

Esther 4:13-14
".....Do not think in your heart that you will escape in the king's palace any more than all the other Jews.
For if you remain completely silent at this time, relief and deliverance will arise for the Jews from another place, but you and your father's house will perish.

Yet who knows whether you have come to the kingdom for such a time as this?"

Mordecai's words spoke volumes. Perhaps Esther was in the kingdom for *"such a time as this."* Esther also knew it was time for her to live out her purpose. She sent word to her cousin Mordecai to gather all the Jews in the area of Shushan and asked them do go on a three- day fast on her behalf. She and her maids also would fast for three days and nights. Esther was going to enter into the courts without being called by the king. It was against the law and she knew how dangerous it would be as she said, *"...And so I will go to the king, which is against the law; and if I perish, I perish!" Esther 4:16*

The king later sees the beautiful Queen Esther standing in the courts dressed in her royal robes. He sent for her. She had found favor with the king. She wasn't put to death for being there uninvited. The king asked what Queen Esther desired.

When you live a life of nobility, honor, and respect, the Lord will bless you too with your heart's desire. Like Queen Esther, many of us are in divine position to commune with the King. Esther invited the king to a banquet. Before seeing the king, Esther prayed and fasted. She was so wise to go before God prior to going before the king. Esther did not make her request immediately. Instead, Esther invited the king to a second banquet so that she had the perfect opportunity to ask for the lives of the Jews.

Queen Esther asked to spare the lives of the Jews. The king granted her wish.

Queen Esther was a Kingdom dweller for a special purpose. She became a hero to many.

Esther 5:3
"And the king said to her, " what do you wish,
Queen Esther?
What is your request? It shall be given to you,
up to half the kingdom"

We are Kingdom dwellers for such a time as this! Learn how to enter the Lord's presence with the beauty of holiness. Learn how to worship Him, obey Him, and be willing. You will be blessed beyond your imagination!

Word vs. World
Improve Your Self-esteem and Self-worth

Who was Queen Esther exactly? She was just another young virgin in the community before she came to live in the palace. She was obedient and courageous. She became a Queen and a hero to many. It still amazes me how the Lord uses weaker vessels to do His mighty work. This is why I appreciate the Word so much. The Bible is filled with stories of humble, common everyday people who become mighty and victorious for the sake of God.

Knowing the Word of God is essential. The Bible is filled with the promises of God and His very thoughts and plans for our lives. We can then differentiate what the Word says versus what the world says. Living a lifestyle of celibacy will require you to know the difference.

The world will tell you that you are not royalty and that you are not special, beautiful, or even worthy. The world will tell you that you will never amount to anything. The world will continue to fill your mind with lies. You need to guard yourself from those lies.

I'll never forget the time a man I dated told me that he was the best thing that ever happened to me. He went on to tell me that I would never find another man who would wait for me until marriage. Those words hurt me, but I proved him wrong. I had a better opinion of myself than he did. He was not the best thing that ever happened to me. He was in my life for a season and I am thankful for that chapter of my life being closed.

Problems come when you start falling for the lies of this world. When you start believing the world's view, you fail to see yourself as a King's kid. You allow the world to set the standards for your life and make a determination of "who" you are. The devil is a liar. We are to focus on what God says. Therefore know the Word.

The world's view of who you are is drastically different from what the Word says. If you fail to see who you are in the sight of the Lord our King, you may suffer from low self-esteem and low self-worth. Unfortunately some of us don't realize how much we are worth to the Lord. People who have low self-esteem will even allow for people to mistreat them. Perhaps this is why Tammy stayed in her damaging relationship.

To have a positive self-esteem means to have confidence and respect of self. To have positive self-worth is to have much value or worthiness of self. Whenever I think about the royal kingdom, I see people of great respect and honor. I can't imagine a princess being talked to negatively in the royal courts or otherwise. People of noble character are self assured, assertive, and respectable people. No one is going to pushover the princess!

Why than do so many of us allow people to mistreat us? So many times, I've watched my friends enter relationships that were abusive, unhealthy, and unfruitful. Many were abused (verbally, physically, and emotionally). Why did they stay? Better yet why didn't they demand the respect and the honor due to them? Perhaps they weren't acting like noble women or perhaps they didn't know how loved they were by God. Maybe they were afraid to be single. What happened to their self-worth?

I believe that we as women are more sensitive than men when it comes to self-esteem, self worth, self-image, and body image. Unfortunately, our society (the world) has produced an image of the perfect shape and size. Many females believe they have to conform to what society says. These worldly images are false images. The world can't tell you who you need to be or who you are, but the Word can.

Magazine advertisements or even commercials should never make us feel ugly, unattractive, and useless. Many of the models we see are being exploited and are being used as sex symbols. Did the Lord ever say that we had to be 36-24-36? Where is that written? Men may be attracted to women who are barely dressed, but do you think men can truly respect these women?

Please don't allow society (the world) fool you into believing that you have to play a harlot to be attractive. You are already beautiful. A good man will look beyond your outward appearance and search for something more meaningful — your spirit. A good man is looking for a humble woman with a God-fearing spirit that his own spirit can recognize. You should want the same in a man. You should want a man who has the spirit of God, and one who is open and obedient to the Lord. It's wonderful to have the Lord love you through your mate. That is exactly what I look forward to.

In singleness, young women need to build themselves up in the Lord to increase their courage, self-esteem, faith, and self worth. These qualities will increase you and prepare you to do all that the Lord has purposed for you in singleness. In singleness, know that you have a great opportunity to be all that you can be in Christ.

Reflection story

This is one of my greatest life lessons. When I was a teenager, I experienced a bad relationship. I endured verbal abuse, which led to an emotional breakdown and depression. At that particular time, I did not know "who" I was in Christ.

The world was lying to me about who I was. The man I was dating tried to tell me who he thought I was. According to him, I was never pretty enough or smart enough. Low self-esteem and low self-worth was inevitable at this point.

It only took one person to bring me that low! After several months in the relationship, I knew I needed out. All of his distorted thoughts of me had driven me to the edge Enraged, I ended the relationship. My self-esteem was so low, however, that I actually asked him back! It appeared as if my decision to end the relationship actually hurt his feelings, and he was no longer willing to be in a relationship with me again.

I am so happy that he didn't want me back. The relationship was obviously unfruitful and unhealthy. He was a good person however; he wanted me to be someone that I was not meant to be. Unfortunately at that point in my life, I was unable to see what God saw in me. All I could see was what this man was showing me about myself, which were all lies. This man was trying to change me to fit whatever standards the world had for women.

Princesses, this is why it's so important to know who you are in Christ. You are fearfully and wonderfully made! Haven't you ever felt like one of God's favorites? Well if not, know that you are. Any relationship that is unhealthy, hindering, and unfruitful needs to end. If that man is breaking you down mentally, spiritually and emotionally, please let it go. If that person is not lifting you in the spirit, please let it go. If you ever question who you are to Christ, know that you are worth more than the price of rubies, princess! You deserve to be treated like the royal one that you are!

Prayer

From this day forward, I want to see myself as You see me.

According to Your Word, I am fearfully and wonderfully made.

There are no mistakes about me. I am Yours and You made me beautiful.

When insults and negativity come my way, I will not receive it.

When my walk of celibacy becomes difficult I pray that I will remember Your promises, You are with me always. You know everything about me, my uprising and down sitting.

Thank You for Your Word.

CHAPTER 4

Question Four:
What Is the Benefit
of Being Single?

Celebrate Singleness!

I will never forget the time I spoke at a youth conference and one of the girls challenged me about being single. The teenager said, "Being celibate means being single so what is so good about being single. I don't want to be without a man!"

My first reaction was to laugh. I mean, where did this child get the nerve to ask about being without a man. Then I thought if this little 14-year-old thinks this way, then what do most adults think about? Who told this little girl that she needed a man to be happy? What made her think that single-ness was a bad thing?

In my work with teenaged girls and young women, I have observed that many of us who suffer from low self-esteem and low self-image are also afraid of being single. Perhaps we believe that not having "somebody" makes us a "nobody." This is why some of us hang on to unproductive relationships. Some of us may feel as if the other person is our world, our source, and our everything. We tend to put that boyfriend on a pedestal. We tend to think so highly of them and less of ourselves.

Know that singleness is a gift from God. Singleness is to be celebrated. When you are single, you have the opportunity to worship the Lord wholeheartedly. The Lord is to be number one in your life. Apostle Paul said:

I Corinthians 7:34
"...There is a difference between a wife and a virgin.
The unmarried woman cares about the things of the Lord,
that she may be holy both in body and in spirit.
But she who is married cares about the things of the world,
how she may please her husband."

The Single Survey

Tell me exactly what do you think of yourself? Are you attractive, friendly, intelligent, witty etc. Use your own words to describe who you are.

_____ _____ _____ _____

_____ _____ _____ _____

_____ _____ _____ _____

List positive things about yourself. My strengths include:

_____ _____ _____

_____   _____   _____

List negative things about yourself or the things you would like to change. My weaknesses are:

_____   _____   _____

_____   _____   _____

Now after listing all of the negative things, do you love yourself? _____
Have you ever allowed a person to hurt you, mistreat you, hit you, belittle you, manipulate you, lie to you, or disrespect you? _____

If so, why? _____
Have you ever stood up for yourself? _____
If so, how did it make you feel? _____
Are you ready to make changes in your life? _____
Are you ready to be bold in Jesus' name? _____
Are you ready to love yourself and who you are in Christ?

_____

Surely you know what it is like to feel good about yourself. So you must know how good it feels to be respected. There is so much power gained when you demand to be respected. One should never compromise themselves or their beliefs. Stand firm for what you feel is right.

People Pleaser vs. God Pleaser

Allow me to be the first to say that it is in fact difficult to always do what is right. Living a lifestyle of celibacy produces many challenges. At times I may be strong spiritually but weak physically. There is often a battle between flesh and spirit. The flesh is weak but the spirit is willing.

Galatians 5:16
"...walk in the Spirit, and you shall not fulfill
the lust of the flesh.
For the flesh lusts against the Spirit and the Spirit against
the flesh; and these are contrary to one another, so that you
do not do the things that you wish."

Feeling confident enough to stand up for what's right is a process. Pray for the Holy Spirit to empower you to stay strong. Having positive self-esteem will help you greatly with this process. You must be confident in *who you* are and *whose* you are! This is how you make it!

Personally, my main challenge was losing the title of being a "people pleaser." I had to learn how to be a God pleaser. Even when I started dating, I struggled trying to please men. One date suggested I wear tight clothes. The other wanted me to wear my hair down. One date wanted me to be with him all day long. The other hated when I wore jeans or sneakers. Plenty of my dates begged for sex and/or sexual favors. It's hard to please people. They are never satisfied, you are never good enough, plus you have no abilities to read minds. So how can you expect to please people all the time? You can't do it. I'd rather please God. Life for me is much easier as a God pleaser. Do you realize how hard it is to please people?

By no means should you feel the need to please men in order to be loved. The truth is that you are already loved. The Lord will not withhold any good thing from you. You are His child. The Lord loves you and wants to give you all good things.

Psalms 84:11
"...The Lord will give grace and glory;
No good thing will He withhold
from those who walk uprightly."

God is able to do anything but fail. Please don't put all your trust in man, but please God by believing in Him. Having faith in God pleases Him

Psalms 84:12 "Blessed is the man who trusts in You!"

Trust God to be your Source. This will prevent you from putting men on a pedestal way above yourselves. We make the mistake of putting our faith, trust, and hope in man. Whenever we put a man on a pedestal those men become idols to us. We should never put anyone or anything before the Lord. We are to worship God only, not man.

II Corinthians 11:2
For I am jealous for you with godly jealousy.
For I have betrothed you to one husband,
that I may present you as
a chaste virgin to Christ.

I have included ten essentials for you to remember and consider in your walk of celibacy.

Remind yourself daily of "who" you are in Jesus. It is a blessing to be single.

1) Discover who you are.
You are a child of God. Remind yourself of this daily. Meditate on how beautifully and wonderfully made you are. God made you and created you beautifully. Don't forget His love for you. The Lord loves you forever.

Jeremiah 31: 3
"...Yes, I have loved you with an everlasting love;
Therefore with loving kindness I have drawn you."

2) Recognize your purpose. Single women have a divine purpose.

I Corinthians 7:34
"...The unmarried woman cares about the things
of the Lord,
that she may be holy
both in body and in spirit."

By discovering your purpose, you tend to be more focused and capable of standing firm during tough and trying times. If you feel as if you don't have a purpose, you are wrong.

Psalms 37:23
"The steps of a good (righteous) man are ordered
by the Lord."

We all have a purpose. Pray and ask the Lord to show you your purpose. Recognize your talents, strengths and goals. Your talents may include singing, writing, witnessing, speaking, painting, or playing an instrument. Whatever your talents may be, try to develop them. Recognize your weaknesses as well. Let those weaknesses become your new challenge. Strive to improve on each one. For example, if a weakness includes falling to peer pressure, then pray that you find the strength to stand for what you believe so that you will not give into peer pressure.

II Corinthians 12:9
"..My grace is sufficient for you: for My strength is made
perfect in weakness"

3) Realize that the way you live your life is a reflection of your faith and love for the Lord. Your singleness gives you the opportunity to minister in so many ways. Your character is a reflection of your spirit. We are called *"the light of the world" Matthew 5:14.* When you have the Lord's spirit, you have His light. Don't let anyone put out your light.

Matthew 5:16
"Let your light so shine before men, that they may see your good works and glorify your Father in heaven."

4) Repeat these words everyday. *"I can do all things through Christ who strengthens me!" (Philippians 4:13).* When you have the Spirit of God in you, you have His power and His strength.

5) You are created in His image and God does not make any mistakes. God can do anything but fail. God has a divine purpose and plan for your life. You are His workmanship!

Ephesians 2:10
For we are, His workmanship, created in Christ Jesus for good works, which God prepared beforehand that we should walk in them.

6) God has always loved you. You were chosen!

Ephesians 1:4
"..just as He chose us in Him before the foundation of the world, the we should be holy and without blame before Him in love."

7) God gives you the right to be His child. He is your Father, your Covering, your Friend, your Everything.

John 1:12
But as many as received Him, to them He gave the right to become children of God, to those who believe in His name.

8) Your union with Christ, not man, makes you complete.

Colossians 2:10
For in Him dwells all the fullness of the Godhead bodily; and you are complete in Him, who is the head of all principality and power.

9) He redeems! If you have lived a life of sin and you believe God can't love you, think again. God redeems!

Ephesians 1:7-8
"In Him we have redemption through His blood, the forgiveness of sins, according to the riches of His grace which He made to abound toward us in all wisdom and prudence..."

When I think of redemption I think of Rahab "the harlot." By no means was she a virgin, chaste and pure. She sold her body in the streets. This same woman, however, was redeemed because of her faith in God.

Hebrews 12:31
By faith the harlot Rahab did not perish with those who did not believe, when she had received the spies with peace.

Rahab knew that God was real. Because of her faith, she acted to assist the men of God. Because of her faith, she was redeemed. *Matthew 1:15*

Ephesians 1:4-8(new creature)

70

Therefore, if anyone is in Christ, he is a new creation;
old things have passed away; behold,
all things have become new.

10) Remember that you are royalty!

I Peter 2:9
"But you are a chosen generation, a royal priesthood, a
holy nation, His own special people, that you may proclaim
the praises of Him who called you out of darkness into His
marvelous light;"

Prayer

*Lord, I pray that I will discover the true beauty
inside myself.*

*I pray that I learn to appreciate the joy of being single for
it gives me the opportunity to worship You without any
distractions.*

*It is my prayer that I can build myself in You
and recognize who I am in You.*

CHAPTER 5

Question 5:
What If My Reputation Is Ruined?

CHARACTER BUILDING and DEVELOPMENT

Colossians 3:12
"Therefore, as the elect of God, holy and beloved,
put on tender mercies, kindness, humility, meekness,
longsuffering;
bearing one another, and forgiving one another....:

Do you know how important it is to improve your character? Your character consists of the qualities that help to distinguish who you are. Your character is your reputation, what people know you for or what people know you to be. Your character represents your moral or ethical strength as well.

Often, someone will ask me about improving his or her reputation after being talked about or rumored to have done some shameful act. The truth is that there is little one can do about the past. Most people take to rumors because it's interesting or exciting. It's good, however, to develop a positive reputation first. When people know the real you or your true character, some rumors simply to stick around.

I realized the importance of developing my character when I first started dating. After meeting one young man, named *Kevin. I was baffled as to why I was so attracted to him. Then I realized it was his character. Kevin was talented, humble, and very hardworking. He was giving, loving, and always helping someone.

I don't remember a time when he was ever being idle. Frequently, I would think of Kevin throughout the day. I figured he was probably busy praying for someone, smiling at someone or encouraging some child. Kevin could be out assisting an elderly person to cross the street, fixing someone's car or sitting in Bible study right now.

You see, I knew Kevin's character, his reputation, and his qualities. Not once did I think he was in a club partying, robbing a bank, or even sneaking around with other women. Kevin's life was an open book filled with tasks and experiences that the Lord had given him. He was out busy using his God-given talents.

Kevin taught me a valuable lesson. What was he thinking about me throughout the day? I decided to develop my own character. I am still working on my character development. The more time I spend with God, the better I become for I become more like Him. (*James 4:8*).

As royalty, we should always work to develop our characters. I wanted to meet good men. I wanted to date men with integrity. Therefore, I needed to be a woman of integrity. Your reputation, personality, and qualities help distinguish who you are and help to shape your character. Here are a few tips and stories to help you develop your character in Christ.

1) Equip yourself with the Word-

II Timothy 3:16-17
"All Scripture is given by inspiration of God, and is profitable for doctrine, for reproof, for correction, for instruction in righteousness, that the man of God may be complete thoroughly equipped for every good work."

The further away we are from the Word, the further away we are from the Truth.

Hosea 4:6 "My people are destroyed for lack of knowledge."

2) Meditate on His Word. Rehearse the scriptures and learn them. The scriptures will become your thoughts, which will allow you to apply the Word to any situation. Each day focus on Jesus, His promises, and all that He is.

Psalm 119:11
"Your word I have hidden in my heart that I might not sin against you."

3) Be obedient to His Word. Princess, there are rules you must follow. The King has spoken. Obey His Word.

Exodus 19:5
"Now therefore, if you will indeed obey My voice and keep My covenant, then you shall be a special treasure to Me above all people; for all the earth is Mine."

4) Be holy! Your conduct is important princess.

I Peter 1:13
Therefore gird up the loins of your mind, be sober, and rest
your hope full upon the grace that is to be brought to you at
the revelation of Jesus Christ;
as obedient children,
not conforming yourselves to the former lusts,
as in your ignorance;
but as He who called you is holy, you also be holy
in all your conduct,
because it is written, "Be holy, for I am holy."

5) Be humble. Humility is beautiful in the sight of the Lord.

1 Peter 5:5-6
" ...and be clothed with humility for
God resists the proud,
But gives grace to the humble"
"Therefore humble yourself under the might hand of God,
that
He may exalt you in due time"

6) Be sober and/or self-controlled. Seeking short-term pleasures could produce a lifetime of consequences. Sobriety
can be defined as seriousness and/or the absence of alcoholic
intoxication. A walk of celibacy requires a serious-minded
person. A person who is sober is self-controlled and serious
about their life and purpose.

1 Peter 5:8
"Be sober, be vigilant;
because your adversary the devil walks about like a roaring
lion,
seeking whom he may devour."

Your role is to be a woman of dignity and class. There is nothing classy about a woman who is drunk, loose, confused, and disoriented. Being sober minded means you are well aware of your actions and your thoughts.

7) Have a joyful spirit. *Rejoice always! (Thessalonians 5:16).* Rejoice and celebrate proclaiming your good news, your faith. You are a celebrating woman. A joyful person represents their thankfulness to God. Please don't walk around telling sad stories about abstinence. A celibate woman is a happy woman with few cares and worries. So continue to celebrate, rejoice and be glad.

8) Be discreet! Discretion shows self-restraint.

Proverbs 4:22
"As a ring of gold in a swine's snout, so is a lovely woman who lacks discretion."

Princess, there is no reason for you to wear skimpy clothes or clothes that barely cover your body. There is no reason for you to dress or act unseemly. Your character is to be classy, sanctified, dignified, and poised. When your outward appearance and attitude are undignified, you no longer represent the Lord. You then represent the world.

9) Be sanctified! Sanctification is holiness and/or purity. In your walk of celibacy, you are a sanctified or dedicated vessel for the Lord. Your purpose is to honor the Lord with your lifestyle of purity. You are set apart from others do to the will of the Lord. You are to be a sanctified, single woman.

II Timothy 2:21
"Therefore if anyone cleanses himself from the latter, he will be a vessel for honor,

sanctified and useful for the Master, prepared for every good work."

If you have lived a lifestyle full of sin, please know that the Lord can forgive, cleanse, redeem, and sanctify you.

I Thessalonians 5:23
"Now may the God of peace Himself sanctify you completely; and may your whole spirit, soul, and body be preserved blameless at the coming of our Lord Jesus Christ."

10) Be chaste, pure, celibate. Why not? Allow your purity to stand out like Rebekah's.

Genesis 24:16
"Now the young woman was very beautiful to behold, a virgin; no man had known her."

She had maintained her purity and she shone radiantly because of it.

11) Pursue righteousness.

II Timothy 2:22
"Flee also youthful lusts; but pursue righteousness, faith, love, peace with those who call on the Lord out of a pure heart."

12) Be committed. To be committed, means to be vowed, promised, or pledged. When you vow to keep yourself for marriage and form an intimate relationship with the Lord, you are obligated to keep your pledge.

Deuteronomy 23:20
"That which has gone from your lips you shall keep and perform, for you voluntarily vowed to the Lord your God what you have promised with your mouth."

Allow your life to become a promise to the Lord. Commit your will, body, spirit, soul, and works to God!

Proverbs 16:3
"Commit your works to the Lord, and your thoughts will be established."

13) Be prepared. You must have the spirit of God!

Matthew 25:7
"Then the kingdom of heaven shall be likened to ten virgins who took their lamps and went out to meet the bridegroom.

"Now five of them were wise, and five were foolish. Those who were foolish took their lamps and no oil with them, but the wise took oil in their vessels with their lamps. But while the bridegroom was delayed, they all slumbered and slept. And at midnight a cry was heard: 'Behold, the bridegroom is coming; go out to meet him! Then all those virgins arose and trimmed their lamps.

And the foolish said to the wise, 'Give us some of your oil, for our lamps are going out.' But the wise answered, saying 'No, lest there should not be enough for us and you; but go rather to those who sell, and buy for yourselves.' And while they went to buy, the bridegroom came, and those who were ready went in with him to the wedding; and the door was shut.

*Afterward the other virgins came also, saying, 'Lord, Lord,
open to us!" But he answered and said, 'Assuredly,
I say to you, I do not know you. "Watch therefore,
for you know neither the day nor the hour in which
the Son of Man is coming."*

In this scripture, the oil represents the Spirit of the Lord.
The foolish virgins were ill prepared; they started out on
their destination without their Source. Before you start out
on your faith walk of celibacy, make sure you have your
Source, the Spirit of the Lord.

14) Be diligent. Living a lifestyle of celibacy, you need to
have a diligent character. Persevere through all of your trials
and continue to press toward the high mark. Continue to
pursue righteousness.

*II Timothy 2:15
Be diligent to present yourself approved to God, a
worker who does not need to be ashamed, rightly
dividing the word of truth.*

15) Be virtuous and be respected. Now, don't think that just
because you are a daughter of the King means that you are
automatically a woman of virtue. You have to live the life
of a virtuous woman. Be respected. You have to develop
a character of great stature, purity, classiness, dignity, and
excellence. This must be achieved so you can easily be
considered a woman of virtue, a woman of moral excellence
and goodness.

*Ruth 3:11
"And now, my daughter, do not fear.
I will do for you all that you request, for all the people of
my town know that you are a virtuous woman."*

Reflection story

A few years ago, I was working at a university. Many of the students there were also in the military. I befriended two extremely well mannered and well-groomed service men, Luke and Ellis. These men taught me a lot. Both were married with children and both shared a strong faith in God.

Luke would share stories and pictures of his beautiful wife and children. He spoke of how he met his wife, loved her dearly, and wanted to respect her. Luke indeed respected his wife and decided not to sleep with her prior to marriage. When I heard this, my soul rejoiced. What a man! It's not everyday that you hear of a husband loving the Lord and his wife so dearly.

The respect that Luke has for his wife was so encouraging to me that I thought, "God, if you could do it for his wife, Tracey, then you can do it for me!" His story was a great inspiration.

Months later, I spoke to his wife over the phone. You guessed it; she had a beautiful character. She was extremely charming and delightful. You could tell the she had the Spirit of God by her very character over the telephone! What a couple! What a union! The Lord works just like that. He is the ultimate matchmaker! He put Luke and Tracey together without a doubt. I knew that I would one day meet my very own prince like Luke.

Luke encouraged me with his personal story. His commitment to God sustained me, giving me hope that there were in fact good men out there who still believed in the things of God and were willing to wait.

Months later, just when I needed another dose of the God's Greatest Moments, I heard another powerful story from my other buddy, Ellis. Ellis blessed me when I needed it the most. I was going through a difficult time after a breakup with a boyfriend of three years. When I found out Ellis was graduating and leaving the university, I went to say goodbye to him. He gave me a wonderful compliment.

After we exchanged pleasantries, he did something I would not have expected. He asked about my boyfriend. I was perfectly honest with him and told him about the breakup and about my faith. In a roundabout way I told him about my decision to wait to experience sex in marriage, let the boyfriend go, and continue to wait for marriage.

Ellis told me that my ex-boyfriend was foolish to pass me up. He described me as being a virtuous woman. That description alone nearly sent me shouting. He also told me that when my *"husband"* finds me that he would find a good thing and would never let me go.

Proverbs 18:22
" He who finds a wife finds a good thing, and obtains favor from the Lord"

Ellis went on to tell me about his own wife. He had been married before and had not planned on marrying again. He was stationed in what he called a "party town" and was eager to find a companion to date while he was stationed there. He would go to the nightclubs but would always feel "empty" or disappointed. The clubs simply did not have what he wanted.

One day he met this woman. She was lovely, delicate and she was saved. She was not a party girl. She was good, decent, classy, and a virgin. She was a virtuous woman!

He fell for her big time!

She is now "Mrs. Ellis," and they are totally in love with each other. He spoke so highly of his wife and how the Lord gave her to him. He knew that God definitely gave him a virtuous woman, a gift, a treasure. Ellis will continue to serve God fervently till the end of time because of the favor given to him. That story, those compliments reminded me of the Proverbs 31 woman.

Proverbs 31:10
"Who can find a virtuous wife?
For her worth is far above rubies"

Ellis taught me that I did not have to change "who" I really was because the Lord will provide me with my prince. As Ellis would say,

" When your husband finds you, he will find a good thing
and

he will not let you go!"

Ladies, desire to be called a virtuous woman! Desire to be thought of as a respected woman of God. Keep your character of royalty. Desire to be considered the jewel in your husband's crown. Desire to be a virtuous woman, a gift and a treasure.

Who can find a virtuous woman?
Proverbs 12:4

"An excellent wife is the crown of her husband..."

A good woman is a treasure!

Prayer

Show me how to walk in Your ways, Lord.
Teach me how to be more like You.
Humble me Lord, when I act like I am better than others.
Quiet me Lord, when my mouth says the wrong things.
Prepare me Lord, for this journey. Give unto me Your Spirit
so that I can continually pull from my Source.
Sanctify me.
Cleanse me, Lord.
Keep me, Lord.
I trust You, Lord.
I will continue to diligently seek You

CHAPTER 6

Question 6: Am I of Any Value?

TREASURES

"Every good gift and every perfect gift is from above,
and comes down from the Father of lights...."
(James 1: 17)

Ellis found a treasure, a virtuous woman, his wife. Luke's wife found a true gem as well, her husband Luke, a faithful man of God. What's a treasure to you? Is there anyone that you treasure? Do you consider yourself a treasure?

Treasure according to The American Heritage Dictionary is defined as:

" 1) Accumulated or stored wealth in the form of money,
jewels, or other valuables.
2) One considered esp. precious or valuable. "

To treasure something means to store away, save up, or hoard for future use. When you treasure something or someone you value them greatly. In a youth seminar a teenager once asked me if she was of any worth. After speaking to her mother at the function, I discovered that the girl was pregnant. She felt worthless because her unplanned pregnancy caused her parents great pain. She was ridiculed by her friends and dumped by the baby's father. She was embarrassed by her situation and felt ashamed. When she approached me, she pulled me away from everyone and asked how God saw sinners. I was surprised by the question. So I went on to tell her that the love of God went beyond her situation and that she was worth the price of rubies to Him. She looked at me puzzled and asked, "Am I of any value?" This young girl reminded me of a story I once heard about a speaker who held up a twenty-dollar bill in the air and asked students to raise their hands if they wanted it. Everyone raised their hands. The speaker then crumbled the bill and then asked the students, "Who wants it now?" Everyone still raised their hands. The speaker then threw the bill down grinding it into the ground making it dirty and filthy, and then asked, "Who wants it now?" Everyone raised their hands. The speaker then explained that the value of the bill never changed despite being crumpled, dropped, and dirtied. The speaker told the group that regardless of how many times they had been crumpled, dirtied, and dropped, their value stayed the same to those who loved them. I took a lot from this story. Regardless of the sin I am in or the mess I just came out of, I will never lose my value. My worth is the very same. We are still wanted, needed, and loved.

You will always be a treasure to God. You are His vessel! You are valued greatly by Him.

You are His precious one!

If you can name 10 things you treasure, list right beside that the reason why you treasure them.

_____   _____
_____   _____
_____   _____
_____   _____
_____   _____
_____   _____
_____   _____
_____   _____
_____   _____

My list is as follows:

Loved ones
God's unfailing love
Salvation
Knowing the will of God
Health/strength
Abilities/talents
Devotional time
Relationship with the Lord
Holy Spirit/Holy Spirit
My (virginity)

Treasure One: Loved ones such as family, because they have shown me love unconditionally. They introduced me to the Lord. My friends have prayed for me, supported me, and interceded for me. Most of all they reinforce my faith in Christ.

Treasure Two: God's unfailing love is such a treasure to me because no matter what I have done or didn't do, He still loves me and desires good things for me.

Treasure Three: Salvation is a given. I am thankful for having the Lord in my life and for His precious gift of salvation. This is a treasure that I could only repay by being obedient to the will of God. Jesus the Son of God was sent here for a divine purpose. He was to bring Salvation to a world full of sinners. Because God so loved the world, He gave His son Jesus to us (John 3:16)

Treasure Four: Knowing the will of God is a huge treasure to me. Without knowing God's will, I wouldn't know where to go, what to do, and how to handle life's ups and downs. Knowing the will of God for your life is what keeps you. It helps you to live your life on purpose.

Treasure Five: My health and strength is essential. I know what it feels like to be ill, tired and weak. *Nehemiah 8: 10 "...for the joy of the Lord is your strength."*

Treasure Six: Thank God for my abilities and strengths. For over ten years, I worked in nursing homes, clinics and hospitals. I experienced working with people with severe disabilities. Some of my clients couldn't bathe themselves, go to the restroom without assistance, nor feed themselves. So with my God-given talents and abilities, I want to bless others.

Treasure Seven: Devotional spending time showing love, affection, and undivided attention to the Lord. It could be in the morning before I leave out for work or time I spend later in the day praising and worshiping the Lord. Praying and fasting is another way to show devotion to the Lord. Having time to dedicate to the Lord keeps me rooted and grounded in the Word. Devotional time allows me to stay intimate with the Lord and keeps me in His presence.

Treasure Eight: My relationship with the Lord is a huge treasure to me. The Lord is my very best friend. I don't know where I would be without Him. To know Him is to love Him. Jesus dwells within me. No one can take away this treasure.

Treasure Nine: Having the Holy Spirit is essential. The Holy Spirit has helped me in situations where my flesh was too weak. The Holy Spirit gives me the strength and power to endure, survive and withstand all things. The leading and guidance of the Holy Spirit keeps me. I could do nothing without Him.

II Corinthians 4:7
But we have this treasure in earthen vessels, that
the excellence of the power may be of God and not of us.
Treasure Ten: Last but certainly not least, my virginity is a treasure. I treasure my purity because I am waiting to share this gift with the man the Lord has prepared for me. My decision to wait is a covenant with God, a promise. Waiting is how I want to worship the Lord and glorify Him. I want to sacrifice intimate relationships with men and become intimate with Jesus. My treasure is my life and how I live it for Christ. I love all of my God-given gifts and I treasure them. I guard my treasures because I do not want them ruined, tampered with, or taken away from me. Jesus said,

Matthew 6:19-21
"Do not lay up for yourselves treasure on earth,
where moth and rust destroy and where thieves break in and
steal; but lay up for yourselves treasures in heaven, where
neither moth nor rust destroys and where thieves
do not break in and steal.
For where your treasure is, there your heart will be also."

For those of you who wrote ten treasures and you listed a lot of material things, just imagine if someone stole them from you. Wouldn't you feel violated? Better yet, how would you feel if you lent someone one of your ten items, and they broke it, damaged it or just simply did not take good care of "your treasure?" What if you gave it to someone and you wish you hadn't? How would you feel? Now, imagine if one of your treasures was a gift from God. Would you let someone borrow it? What if you lost the treasure?

Luke 14:8
"Or what woman, having ten silver coins, if she loses one coin, does not light a lamp, sweep the house, and search carefully until she finds it?
And when she has found it, she calls her friends and neighbors together, saying, Rejoice with me, for I have found the piece which I lost!"

Losing a treasure causes sadness but imagine giving away a treasure away and living to regret it? One of the worst feelings one could have is regretting a decision that causes one to lose so much, a priceless, irreplaceable, treasure.

Remember that Jesus said,

"Do not give what is holy to the dogs; nor cast your pearls before swine, lest they trample them under their feet, and turn and tear you in pieces."
Matthew 7:6

Don't give away your precious treasures to those who are unworthy, those who are looking for a temporary thrill, and those who don't truly know you nor to those who don't care about you. An undeserving person hurts, uses, and abuses you. Do you remember the story of Esau? Esau gave away his precious gift, his birthright (inheritance) for a temporary fulfillment. We have to remember how much could be lost for temporary fulfillment or pleasure. Why would someone mistreat the holy things of God for a temporary thrill?

Hebrews 12:16-17
Lest there be any fornicator or profane person like Esau, who for one morsel of food sold his birthright.
For you know that afterward, when he wanted to inherit the blessing,
he was rejected, for he found no place for repentance,

though he sought it diligently with tears.

For bread and lentil soup, Esau sold his birthright to his brother. When his flesh was fulfilled, he rose and left! When he wanted to be blessed, he was rejected for he had given his gift away. Esau felt horrible for his carelessness and instead of repenting, he became angry with his brother.

Be careful not to give away your precious treasures to those undeserving. The birthright was meant for Esau because he was firstborn. Meaning that, the firstborns were to receive a double blessing rather than the next child. Esau gave up his blessing, a priceless treasure!

Only for God would I give up my precious treasures. Only for Him am I willing to lose my own life. Only for the Lord am I willing to labor and to give my all. The Lord is deserving of all that I have. Without Him, I would not be nor would I have anything. Therefore, I am a steward of all the things that the Lord has given me because they belong to Him anyway. So, in the meantime, my ministry, life, and my body, I will honor and protect because they ultimately belong to the Father.

I Corinthians 6:19
Or do you not know that your body is the temple
of the Holy Spirit who is in you, whom you have from God,
and you are not your own?

We are to be good stewards of what the Lord has given to us. This includes our bodies.

"Blessed is that servant whom his master will find so doing
when he comes!"
Luke 12:43

The Lord requires all of us to be good stewards but what if He instructed us to release one of our treasures. What if one of your treasures is a relationship with a boyfriend?

Do you think you could walk away from someone that you love and cherish?

I did!

Reflection story

Sacrificing a treasure for a much greater, everlasting gift. Years ago I was in a relationship. The Lord was leading me to "let it go," however, I was not yet willing to give up the relationship. You must understand, I thought I was in love. At this time in my life, this young guy was all that I knew about dating. I thought he was special and that there would never be another man like him in my life again.

My poor mother must have heard hundreds of stories about this young man for I was truly smitten by him. Then one night my mother told me a story that changed my life.

She spoke of a young pastor she knew. The man, not yet a pastor, was deeply in love with a very beautiful woman. The man desired the things of the Lord. He wanted the Holy Spirit. Something was hindering him from obtaining a greater walk with Jesus. My mother remembers him praying in church and shouting out loud, "I don't want her, Lord...I don't want her." He had to get that woman out of his life in order to get to his rightful place in Jesus.

This beautiful woman had been an obstacle for the young preacher. She may have been a beautiful person but was she meant for him? Perhaps, the Lord spoke to him concerning this woman but like myself, he held onto her. He couldn't let her go until he realized the worth of serving God with his whole heart and having the spirit of God was far better than having the woman in his life.

The young preacher did finally marry and is still married to this day. This story was an inspiration for me because at that point in my life I wanted the things of God. I wanted to feel His presence and to have His love. My mother said to me very clearly, "Don't tell the Lord you don't want this man if you really do." It did not take long for me to make my decision. After all, I wanted to be with this young man but not nearly as much as I wanted God.

That night I went into my room and told the Lord, "I don't want him Lord, I want you." I cried myself to sleep that night but still deep in my heart, I was satisfied. I knew I had God. Months later after I cried out to God with my sacrifice, I was *still* pining for this young man. What was wrong with me?

One Sunday my church traveled to visit another church in the country. The music was beautiful, praises filled the room, and the wonderful testimonies were setting people on fire. The Spirit of God was in that place. No doubt about it, He was there! When it was time for an altar call, I wanted to get in line.

In line for an altar call, I told the pastor that I wanted to pray for my family. I thought about the young man I had been pining for, but I was too ashamed to ask for help releasing an old boyfriend.

With lifted hands, the pastor started to speak. I started to pray in the Spirit extremely loud. My body started to move without me initiating movement. I was set on fire from on high. The pastor looked toward my pastor and said, "The Holy Spirit is all over this child." One woman said to me "The Lord wants you to let go of whatever you are holding onto. The Lord says, "Let It Go!"

Can you believe that! The Lord revealed my problems to these ladies. I got my confirmation that Sunday. So, do you think I listened? No, not right away. I questioned what the woman had told me.

A few days later, I went to pick up a few girls from church to go shopping. While waiting for one of the girls, I started talking to one of the sisters from church. I told her about the church service when the woman said for me to "let go." I asked, "What do you think she means?" The sister looked at me very seriously and said, "Maybe she is speaking to you about your friend."

Once again, the Lord used someone else to confirm my doubts. At that moment, I "let him go." I gave him up and continued to pray for the Lord to bless him and for the Lord to bless me. The Lord has indeed blessed me! Since letting him go, I received so much!

Abraham and Isaac

Leaving a damaging relationship may be difficult. Releasing your hopes and dreams may be a little harder. However, sacrificing a treasure or a loved one of yours may be unimaginable. Leaving a relationship was hard enough but I had faith. My faith was increased in my obedience. When God instructed Abraham to do the unthinkable and sacrifice his beloved son, Isaac, Abraham obeyed!

Isaac was the son of Sarah, Abraham's precious wife. Isaac was the son Sarah had prayed for. He was given to Abraham and Sarah in their old age. Therefore, Isaac was a miracle, a blessing, and a promise.

Genesis 17:19, 21
Then God said; "No, Sarah your wife shall bear you a son,
and you shall call his name Isaac; I will establish
My covenant with him for an
everlasting covenant, and with his descendants after him."

17: 21
"But My covenant I will establish with Isaac, whom Sarah
shall bear to you at this set time next year."

Abraham is tested!

Genesis 22: 1-3
Now it came to pass after these things that God tested
Abraham, and said to him, "Abraham!"
And he said, "here I am."
Then He said, "Take now your son, your only son Isaac,
who you love,
and go to the land of Moriah,
and offer him there as a burnt offering on one of the moun-
tains of which
I shall tell you.

Genesis 22:3
So Abraham rose early in the morning and saddled his
donkey, and took two of his young men with him, and Isaac
his son; and he split the wood for the burnt offering, and
arose and went to the place of which God had told him.

Are you questioning how a loving father could do such a thing to his son? How could Abraham sacrifice his beloved son Isaac? Now we must consider the relationship that Abraham and God had. It was intimate! God and Abraham had made promises to one another. Abraham had a covenant with his Heavenly Father. Perhaps we should think of God's great sacrifice. God gave His only begotten Son, Jesus. Jesus was sent to earth to die so that we might live. Jesus went through with His death knowing that His death would benefit us. He gave His life for us.

Abraham obeys!

Abraham placed his son on the altar and took out the knife to slay his son. Then an Angel of the Lord stopped him. *"Abraham, Abraham!"*

"Do not lay your hand on the lad, or do anything to him; for now I know that you fear God, since you have not withheld your son, your only son, from Me." Genesis 22:11-12

Abraham is blessed!

Abraham was provided with a ram in the bush to sacrifice in place of his son. The Angel of the Lord continue to speak to him saying,

Genesis 22:16-18
"By Myself I have sworn, says the Lord,
because you have done this thing,
and
have not withheld your son,
your only son—

Blessing I will bless you,
and multiplying I will multiply your descendants
as the stars of the heaven and as the sand which
is on the seashore;
and your descendants shall possess the gate
of their enemies.

In your seed all the nations of the earth shall be blessed,
Because
you obeyed My voice."

I pray that these scriptures will encourage you to cherish your true treasures, especially your priceless relationship with the Lord. Forming an intimate relationship with the Lord, gives you the ability to trust Him enough to put your all on the altar. When the Lord desires for you to release an unfruitful relationship, status, fast lifestyle, and/or a career, I pray that you will obey His voice and be blessed.

When you love the Lord and are intimate with Him, you can find peace obeying His word! Honor your God-given talents, treasures and the Word of God.

> *...Whoever is of a willing heart, let him bring*
> *an offering to the Lord*
> *Exodus 35:5*

You should be willing to give your all to God. Give God all of you. Your gifts, your time, your talents, give them to God. Allow the Lord to use you for a much greater purpose. Trust Him for your life. Trust that He will not withhold any good thing from you.

> *II Corinthians 9:6*
> *"...He who sows bountifully will also reap bountifully."*

Devotion is a beautiful thing in the sight of God. To dedicate your time and energy to Jesus is priceless. I have learned to devote my life to His will. I want to do anything and everything to please the Lord. To devote is to give one's attention, life, time, and self entirely. Also devotion means to set apart for a specific purpose, to vow. I vow my life, my very being to Jesus entirely. I must set myself apart for the specific purpose to praise Him and honor Him in my walk and my talk. My body is for the Spirit of the Lord, and I am His vessel. I give my life to Jesus so He can use me for His will.

> *You were bought at a price;*
> *therefore*
> *glorify God in your body and in your spirit,*
> *which are God's.*
> *I Corinthians 6:20*

Treasure your relationship with God. Abraham put God # 1 in his life. He believed, trusted, and obeyed God. When you live a life of celibacy, you set yourself apart from everyone. You sacrifice temporal pleasures for an eternal friendship with Jesus. To sacrifice a little to gain so much more is easy. Please God in your walk and talk. Honor Him with your obedience. Please Him with your very life.

Living a life of celibacy requires obedience, faith in God and surrendering of your own will. You are a treasure to God, the jewel in His crown. If you value your own life, you value Jesus. Your body is not your own, you were bought with a price. When Jesus died, He purchased you. You are priceless to Him. He gave His very life for you and He loves you, and will do anything for you. Always remember that you are His treasure, His vessel. Therefore, let all your thoughts and praises be toward your Lord and Savior.

Psalms 19:14
Let the words of my mouth and the meditation of my heart
Be acceptable in Your sight,
O Lord, my strength and my Redeemer."

Prayer

Lord, help me to recognize that You are my Everything.
You are my beloved Treasure.
I pray that I never despise, damage, or neglect any treasures that You have given me.
Lord, I thank You for all of Your precious gifts and treasures such as Your spirit, love, peace, wisdom, word, faithfulness, protection, mercy, grace, and strength.
I ask that You continue to bless me with these treasures and continue to remind me daily of my many blessings.

I ask, Lord, that You will help increase my awareness of my blessings, so that I may be forever thankful for all You do.
I thank You for the things You have done for my life and the things You will do.

PART II

I Want To Be With A Man Now, Why Wait?

CHAPTER 7

Question 7:
Why Can't We Have Sex Now?

SLOW DOWN
Don't Be So Anxious!

Philippians 4:6

A popular question I receive from young people every-where is "Why can't I have sex if all of my other friends have?" The truth is, many of their friends aren't having sex or if they are having sex, they lie about their experiences. Many lie to gain attention. Many tell people that their experience was wonderful and exciting to cause their friends to be envious. Don't worry or be anxious about rushing into life or rushing into a sexual experience. As a young woman on a mission to please the Lord, men will come out of the woodwork for you. Men will try their hardest to be with you. Don't rush in. Don't let anyone rush you, either. If you are feeling anxious, pressed, rushed, or even lonely, please "slow it down."

At times, life can appear to be moving at the speed of light. Times are changing, people are changing, and our society changes constantly. When life moves real fast, we must hold on to God's unchanging hand. We have to become settled and anchored in the Lord. When everything seems to be spinning out of control, we need to slow down and take control.

When we rush anything, mistakes are bound to happen. One of my favorite television shows was "I Love Lucy." One episode, Lucy and her friend, Ethel, started a new job at a candy factory. The little candies were coming toward Lucy on a conveyor belt. First the candies came at a good pace, which was nice and slow, just right for Lucy's abilities. After Lucy's boss saw how well she was doing, the boss sped up the machine! The candies were coming down the belt so quickly that Lucy couldn't control the situation. The job became too difficult for her to handle. All the candies she couldn't catch, she tried to eat to get rid of some, shoving many, too many into her mouth. There was no way Lucy could eat the candies she missed. It was entirely too fast for Lucy. She was overwhelmed.

Rushing will cause us to make hasty, irrational decisions. When we rush, we lose focus, forget important things, neglect important people, disregard "the signs," lose sight of our intended path, get sidetracked, and caught up by distractions.

When I was little girl my mother always spoke about how she never received a speeding ticket. She was so proud of her perfect driving record so much that I was proud of her too. I also wanted to have a perfect record. After receiving my license at the age of 16, I had a perfect record for 9 years. Then, one day a county police officer caught me driving nearly 15 miles over the speed limit! What could I say, I was obviously guilty and would have to plead guilty and accept the blemish on my "once perfect" driving record. Well, in my state of residence, a first offense such as this could be cleared if the driver agrees to go to driving school. This will make the offense disappear and no record of the offense will no longer be on record. I thought to myself, "yes, I have one chance to wipe this slate clean and it will be just like new again." I can now start all over and try to keep the not-so-perfect record perfect for now.

Honestly, I felt that the Lord allowed the police to catch me "speeding." I truly felt that it was time for me to slow down, not just in my driving, but also in my way of living. My lifestyle was moving way off course and way out of control. I was living recklessly. That ticket not only hurt my feelings, but it caught my attention. I learned an important message from this incident and decided I needed to take some of my own advice. Slow down! Please be patient with your life experiences. Don't rush growing up. Wherever you want to go or whatever you want to do, keep God in mind. Put Him first. Pray over the situation and proceed with caution.

Thinking back to that time in my life, I was foolishly spending money, hanging out with a bad crowd, talking too much to too many people. Unfortunately, with all the things I was doing, I wasn't praying like I used to, nor was I truly acknowledging what the Lord had done for me. I wasn't always obedient to God. It was time to slow down.

Philippians 4:6
"Be anxious for nothing, but in everything by prayer and supplication, with thanksgiving, let your requests be made known to God."

At that time in my life, I was headed for something awful. The road I was traveling on was headed for destruction; however, the Lord warned me with a small incident such as this. After the incident, I admitted guilt, repented, and moved on carefully. Sometimes the Lord will allow things to happen and/or even send someone in your direction to help you, support you, and even warn you.

My slate was wiped clean just one time with this first offense. What if I got another offense? I would not be so fortunate. With Jesus, we have continual grace and mercies. We repent and try our best not to offend and the Lord keeps wiping our slates clean. He places all sins in the sea of forgetfulness. Our God is a merciful God.

What an awesome God we serve. I am so glad to have a Father like Him. He still loves me and on top of all that He forgives, warns me and slows me down so that I can recognize Him and recognize my sinful ways.

My speeding could have resulted in an accident. What if a child was crossing the street in the path of my speeding car or what if I had struck another vehicle? Why was I in such a hurry? Why do we rush our life experiences? Why worry and be so anxious?

"Do not be anxious about anything,"

It's important to pray about all things because you should want the Lord with you in all things. I want to be blessed in every situation and I don't want to take anything for granted nor fail to recognize God.

Psalm 19:14
"Let the words of my mouth and the meditation of my heart
Be acceptable in Your sight,
O Lord, my strength and my Redeemer.

The Fast Life

I have had the opportunity to work at elementary schools through high schools. For two years I even taught at a university. Some of the things I heard and saw at these establishments sickened me. There are children ages 10 and 11 that are already involved with sexual activities. Turn on any talk show and you will see horror stories of young ladies who want to rush into adult experiences. These youngsters are frequenting clubs, attempting to become strippers, pursuing married men, having babies, aborting babies, abandoning babies, and becoming prostitutes. This is not just something we may watch on television any more. These people are our neighbors, co-workers' children, and family members. No way am I trying to condemn anyone, but I am trying to encourage young ladies to live a more satisfactory lifestyle.

There are college students who are sneaking into male dorms participating in orgies and wild parties. There are rapes and attacks reported on a weekly basis. Some of these young girls were being walked home from a party drunk and incoherent. They were taken advantage of because they were simply not sober nor sober minded.

Living a life of celibacy is beneficial as well as safe. Perhaps if these girls had their minds made up that they would not participate in such fast living, they would not have suffered so greatly during their young lives. I pray for these young women and their families.

Living a fast lifestyle will lead you into destruction. Most youngsters have no idea what lies waiting. When you live fast you risk contracting STD's, HIV/AIDS, addictions, soul-ties, and you open the door wide open for the enemy to enter.

Even when these youngsters are not sexually active, they are trying to experiment with drugs and alcohol. Life is not all fun and games. Living this way does not solve any problems. It's another temporary fix that can cause you to experience a lifetime of hurt.

A word of caution to those living too fast; there is an enemy out there who desires to sift you like wheat. One moment in a drunken stupor or a few drags of some experimental drug can open the doors to the enemy. In an instant, your whole life can be turned upside down.

Luke 22:31
"...Satan has asked for you, that he may sift you as wheat"

I Peter 5:8
"Be sober, be vigilant; because your adversary the devil walks about like a roaring lion, seeking whom he may devour."

The enemy, who is Satan, desires to take your very life, body, spirit, soul, and your mind for his own. You don't belong to the devil. You belong to God. So, please slow down before you get caught up and trapped.

Timing is Everything!

Ecclesiastes 3:1
"To everything there is a season, a time for every purpose under heaven.."

Our way is not like God's ways, nor our timing like His timing. Wait on God's instructions, His will, and His perfect timing for your life. Don't allow anyone to put pressure on you. You are to please God with your life. You owe man nothing. Be a God pleaser and not a people pleaser. (*Ephesians 6:6*).

If you lose friends, the Lord will send you faithful ones. If you are bored because you can't frequent bars and clubs, the Lord will show you a joyful good time. If you so badly want to experience sex, think about the consequences first. In singleness, each person you sleep with may help create a soul tie with you. This means you invited that person's spirits into your life and they attach to your spirit. You could allow demonic spirits into your life that way. I urge you to slow it down.

Just like the local police officer who was waiting for speeding drivers, the enemy is waiting for an anxious female. Setting a speed trap is designed for speeding motorists. The enemy has his own traps and snares for the people of God. He is waiting to trap you and to prevent you from succeeding in life. The enemy desires to take your life. So, for your very life, slow it down! Please be patient and wait on the Lord.

Psalm 27:14
Wait on the Lord;
Be of good courage,
And He shall strengthen your heart;
Wait, I say, on the Lord!

Prayer

Lord, bless my going out and my coming in.

Bless me on this journey. Be with me down every road and every turn.

Teach me to follow after You. Please don't allow me to follow the path of unrighteousness. Lead me into Your way everlasting Lord.

Every hill I must climb, every obstacle I must hurdle, be with me.

The Bible states that the steps of the righteous man are ordered.
Please order each step, Lord.
I pray that You slow me down Lord, when I am being too anxious.
I desire to wait for Your timing.
Keep me moving in the right direction toward safety, peace, and righteousness for Your Name sake.

Amen

CHAPTER 8

Question 8: What Is So Dangerous About Dating?

Beware of TRAPS and COUNTERFEITS

I Peter 5:
" Be sober, be vigilant;
because your adversary the devil walks
about like a roaring lion seeking whom he may devour."

Most teenagers will ask me why dating is dangerous. Being a young woman in this day and time can be difficult. I tell them about the people I dated and how as a teenager, I was naïve, vulnerable and anxious. Just like many of you, I was tempted to rush into life and experience so many things. I hooked up with many counterfeits and fell into numerous traps. Dating can be dangerous if you don't pay attention to the signs. I am so thankful to God that I had Him as my Source. I have made so many mistakes and the Lord kept looking out for me. I was so foolish but God rescued me from danger. I am thankful for the Lord's grace and mercy. He spared me many heartaches, headaches, and harm.

You see the devil desires to steal our joy, peace, and virtue. Do you realize how important it is to rely on the Lord? We need His faith, direction, guidance, strength, and the power of His Spirit. Being anxious or impatient can cause us to lose sight of our destined paths. When we allow ourselves to become distracted, we lose focus and could potentially get lost and easily misled.

When He, the Spirit of truth, has come,
He will guide you into all truth.
John 16:13

Remember to stay on the path that the Lord has set before you and be aware of traps and counterfeits along the way.

Choose the Right Path

Proverbs 7: 4-27
Say to wisdom, "You are my sister, " And call
understanding your nearest kin,
"That they may keep you from the immoral
(strange) woman,
From the seductress who flatters with her words.
For at the window of my house I looked through my lattice,
And saw among the simple, I perceived among the youths,
A young man devoid of understanding, Passing along the
street near her corner;
And he took the path to her house
In the twilight, in the evening,
In the black and dark night.

And there a woman met him,

With the attire of a harlot, and a crafty heart.
She was loud and rebellious,
Her feet would not stay at home.
At times she was outside, at times in the open square,
Lurking at every corner.
So she caught him, and kissed him;
With an impudent face said to him:
I have peace offerings with me;
Today I have paid my vows.
So I came out to meet you,
Diligently to seek your face,
And I have found you.
I have spread my bed with tapestry,
Colored coverings of Egyptian linen.
I have perfumed my bed
With myrrh, aloes, and cinnamon.

Come, let us take our fill of love until
morning; Let us delight ourselves with love.
For my husband (good man) is not at home;
He has gone on a long journey;
He has taken a bag of money with him,
And will come home on the appointed day.
With her enticing speech she caused him to yield,
With the flattering lips she seduced him.

Immediately he went after her, as an ox
goes to the slaughter,

Or as a fool to the correction of the stocks;
Till an arrow struck his liver.

As a bird hastens to the snare,
He did not know it would cost his life.

113

Now therefore, listen to me, my children;
Pay attention to the words of my mouth.
Do not let your heart turn aside to her ways,
Do not stray into her paths;
For she has cast down many wounded,
And all who were slain by her were strong men.
Her house is the way to hell,
Descending to the chambers of death. "

Oh woman of God, please be mindful of this scripture. Although the scripture speaks of a seductress woman, this could very well be a seducing man calling to you! You have no idea what snares and traps are out there. Satan is waiting to trap you and lure you with flattering words. Don't allow yourself to get caught up like this man! He became a victim to the enemy. Pray that you will not fall into temptation. (*Luke 6:13*) If you have strayed onto the wrong path, get off! Don't make wrong choices, hang with immoral people, or do foolish things! This man allowed the enemy to entertain him and change his path. Stay on the path that the Lord has designed for you. Follow Christ.

Society often refers to the youth as being naïve, inexperienced or "devoid of understanding." You may be young and even naïve; however, be warned. Take control of your life and seek the Lord's help. Being knowledgeable of the Word of God will give you direction. Stay off the path of destruction. Understand that there is an enemy out there and he desires to sift you as wheat! Without the Lord in your life, you could easily get trapped.

The harlot in Proverbs had a *crafty heart*. That's just like the devil, full of tricks. Her heart was deceitful and so is the enemy's. This woman represents the type of spirit that desires to destroy you. I used this scripture to demonstrate how the devil works. The man was the victim in this scripture. He made a poor decision.

She was *lurking* around which means she was creeping, lying in wait, ready to ambush someone. Ambush she did. She trapped the man. She *caught* him. She *kissed* him with her *impudent face or in a bold, indiscreet, brash manner.* She *offered gifts* to him. Just like the devil, who seduces with flattering words. He catches you, kisses you, and offers you things.

The devil likes to tempt the children of God this way. Tempting, which is soliciting to sin, usually offers some gift or reward. The reward the devil offers is not worth your life. Trust me, you don't want anything the devil has to offer. Be careful not to fall for the devil's tactics and tricks.

If you notice in the scripture, when the harlot was trying to seduce the man, she was throwing up red flags everywhere. The warning signs were there. She diligently sought after this man. She wanted him. Realize that there are men and women out there who lie in wait for you. They can't wait for you to come near their path of destruction. Who are these people you may ask? These are people who have seducing and demonic spirits just like the harlot on the street.

You have heard the saying, "I bet they saw you coming a mile away." This usually refers to some poor purchase you made or even when someone somehow tricked you. You got played or suckered into something. *And I have found you.* This man was enticed. She saw him coming a mile away.

I have spread my bed with tapestry. Now she is trying to tempt him back to her house, her territory, and her domain. *Come, let us take our fill of love until morning.* She is now giving him an invitation to sin. She is manipulating this unassuming man. He thinks he will sleep with her until the morning if he follows her little scheme.

For my husband is not at home, He has gone on a long journey: will come home on the appointed day. The harlot is married! She is saying, "Hey, the coast is clear." She clearly knows what she is offering is wrong because she is being sneaky. I almost fell for a date's invitation to sneak me into his all-male dorm. The scenario was all wrong. The red flags were there.

With her enticing speech she caused him to yield, with the flattering lips she seduced him. He gave in. *Immediately! Immediately he went after her, as an ox goes to the slaughter...* The scripture says the man immediately or anxiously with great haste or urgency, followed her.

Slow down, fellow, and think about what you are doing!

Sister, if you have a check in your spirit that tells you that your boyfriend or new acquaintance is not right, then don't you go any further. Change your course. Do not follow after him. As for this woman of the street, if you think she was dressed like a harlot, acted like a harlot, and talked like a harlot, she is a harlot. I know we as females may not be able to tell what a man is like from his clothing; however, if you read the previous chapter, we should be wearing clothing of humility. It's spiritual! Girlfriend, check his fruit! Does he have the fruit of the Spirit? *Galatians 5:22-25* If something does not look, feel or sound right, don't go picking! Don't allow him to pick you either. Don't allow the enemy to entertain you that long.

Continue to pray so that the Lord will keep you in your moments of temptation. Pray for the gift of discernment so that when you are approached by brother "so and so," you will know who he really is in the Spirit. It's easier than you think. You just have to be willing to follow after the heart of God and not your own. View the situations through your spiritual eyes. The Lord knows all things and will help you.

"All the ways of a man are pure in his own eyes, but the Lord weighs the spirits." Proverbs 16:2

Be ye warned!

So tell me, what paths will you choose for your life? Most of us would like to raise our hands and say, "Jesus, I plan to follow Jesus!" Even in our walk with Him, the enemy will call out to us in an attempt to persuade us to look his way and entice us.

The devil desires to sift us as wheat, declare war against us Christians, influence us with false philosophies and false teachings, change our path of righteousness, cause us harm, pain, diseases, and ultimately possess the people of God.

Just like the man in Proverbs being led by a woman with a seducing spirit, we too can be easily led the same way. The scripture says that he was being led just like slaughter to the kill, fool in the stocks, caught up in the snares. This example depicts one who is helpless, naïve, and hopeless. Let me assure you that with Jesus you have hope. Choose your friends, your dates, and your paths wisely.

Christians are Satan's number one prey. He desires for you to step off the path of righteousness because once you lose sight of Jesus, the enemy comes in. The enemy is so slick and so sly. He knows your weaknesses. Remember that Satan is a spirit. The enemy wants to entice you with drugs, sex, and idols to disrupt the things of God in your life. Anyway the enemy can distract you, he will. When you turn away from the Lord, you become empty and void. This is when you allow yourself to fall into temptation and the enemy moves right in.

Matthew 12: 43-45
"When an unclean spirit goes out of a man, he goes
through dry places, seeking rest, and finds none.
Then he says, 'I will return to my house from which I came.'
And when he comes, he finds it empty, swept,
and put in order.

*Then he goes and takes with him seven other spirits more
wicked than himself and they enter and dwell there; and the
last state of that man is worse than the first."*

Having the Spirit of God, the oil in your vessel, is the
only way to win against the tactics and tricks of Satan. The
enemy will tempt the people of God in three ways: the lust of
the flesh, the lust of the eyes and the pride of life.

Satan even tried to tempt Jesus on three occasions;
however, Jesus used the Word against the enemy and didn't
fall for the enemy's traps.

Lust of flesh!

Luke 4:1
*Then Jesus, being filled with the Holy Spirit, returned from
the Jordan and was led by the Spirit into the wilderness,
being tempted for forty days by the devil.
And in those days He ate nothing, and afterward,
when they had ended,
He was hungry.
And the devil said to Him, "If you are the Son of God,
command this stone to become bread."*

Here Satan tries to tempt Jesus because He knew that His
flesh was weak. Jesus had been fasting for forty days. The
devil knows our weaknesses too.

But Jesus answered him, saying,

*"It is written, 'Man shall not live by bread alone,
but by every word of God."*

Lust of the eyes!

Luke 4:5
Then the devil, taking Him up on a high mountain, showed
Him all the kingdoms of the world in a moment of time.
And the devil said to Him, "All this authority I will give
You, and their glory; for this has been delivered to me,
and I give it to whomever I wish.
Therefore, if You will worship before me, all will be yours."

The devil tried to offer Jesus instant gratification (glory
and authority) but only if Jesus turned away from God the
Father and serve him. Jesus used the Word again to defeat
the enemy at his own game. The devil lied to Jesus and tried
to manipulate him by offering Jesus the world. Jesus is Lord.
All authority belongs to God anyway.

And Jesus answered and said to him,
"Get behind Me, Satan! For it is written,
You shall worship the Lord your God, and Him only you
shall serve."

Pride of life!

Luke 4:9
Then he brought Him to Jerusalem, set Him on the pinnacle
of the temple, and said to Him, "If You are the Son of God,
throw yourself down from here.
"For it is written: 'He shall give His angels charge over
you, to keep you.'
"and, in their hands they shall bear you up. Lest you dash
your foot against a stone."

The devil is so sly. He is a spirit and he also knows the
Word of God. He would even try distorting the Word of

God to twist the truth. The enemy couldn't win with Jesus, however. Jesus is the Truth, the Light and the Word of God.

And Jesus answered and said to him.
"It has been said, 'You shall not tempt the Lord your God."
Now when the devil had ended every temptation, he
departed from Him until an opportune time.

Do you know how you can resist the enemy like Jesus did?

Matthew 3:16
When He had been baptized, Jesus came up immediately
from the water, and behold, the heavens were opened to
Him and He saw the Spirit of God descending like a dove
and alighting upon Him.

Jesus was equipped with the Spirit of God. You also need to have the Holy Spirit in order to win against the tactics of the devil. Being intimate with the Lord is essential. We must have His Spirit, His word, His will, and His character.

The enemy knows how to corrupt our minds and make people feel inadequate and useless. The devil uses lust of the flesh, lust of the eyes and pride of life to trap the people of God to sin. The enemy knows our human nature. He knows we lust after people, social status, and that we are a very prideful people. We always seem to want what others have. We also like to prove ourselves to others.

Sisters in Christ, in your walk with Jesus and be aware of temptation. Keep the Word hidden in your heart so you do not sin. Be aware of the traps and counterfeits.

Be Ye Careful

Proverbs 23:26 -28

120

My son, give me your heart,
And let your eyes observe my ways.
For a harlot is a deep pit,
And a seductress is a narrow well,
She also lies in wait as for a victim,
And increases the unfaithful among men.

In our bold walk of celibacy, we must have the Spirit of God. God is Love. His love is not tricky or conditional. So many people are easily manipulated by love. So many times in my teenage years, men would say to me, "If you love me, you would sleep with me." The devil is a liar. My answer was always, "If you love me, you will wait." I always knew that those men would never be my future husbands. Their tactics were attempts to manipulate me.

Manipulative people, (men and women) are mentioned all throughout the Bible. Eve was manipulated in the very beginning when the devil tempted her by having her eat the forbidden fruit. Even Esau was tricked and manipulated by his very own flesh and blood, his brother! How about Samson, a mighty and powerful man? He too was manipulated.

Manipulation of love!

Samson was a Nazarite to God. The word Nazarite means promise. Samson's parents were blessed greatly by his miraculous birth, for his mother was barren. His parents were visited by the Angel of the Lord and given specific instructions teaching them ways to care for Samson.

Judges 13:5
For behold, you shall conceive and bear a son. And no razor shall come upon his head, for the child shall be a Nazarite to God from the womb; and he shall begin to deliver Israel out of the hand of the Philistines.

As Samson grew, the Lord blessed him.

Judges 13:25
*"And the Spirit of the Lord began to move upon him at
Mahaneh Dan between Zorah and Eshtaol."*

Samson knew his purpose, yet he fell into temptation.
Samson is a good example of someone who was tremen-
dously blessed by God but was manipulated and trapped by a
seducing spirit that worked through Delilah. The Philistines
offered Delilah money to entice Samson and find out what
made him strong.

Judges 16:5
*"...Entice him, and find out where his great strength lies,
and by what means we may overpower him."*

Samson loved to be in this woman's presence. He would
often rest with her. So it was easy for Delilah to manipulate
him. Many times, she would inquire about Samson's great
strength and its source, but repeatedly Samson teased her and
wouldn't tell her the truth. Not realizing his little game, she
would do whatever she could to bind him up for the Philistines
to capture him. In her frustration, Delilah manipulated Samson
with her tears. Samson had a tender heart for women because
of the tragedy of his first wife. Delilah asked,

Judges 16:15
*"How can you say, 'I love you', when your heart is not with
me? You have mocked me these three times, and have not
told me where your great strength lies."*

Samson cracked under constant pressure from his
lover, Delilah. She finally wears him down and he tells her
everything.

Judges 16:17
"... he told her all of his heart,"
Once the secret was out, Delilah sent for the lords of the
Philistines and told them.

Then she ordered a man to come in to cut his hair after she lulled Samson to sleep on her knees. When the locks were shaved from his head, the Spirit of the Lord had departed him. Samson lost his strength, the anointing of God.

My prayer is for the Lord to please keep me from being manipulated by the enemy and from falling into traps and snares. The last thing I want is to lose the presence of God. The Lord is our strength. I simply couldn't make it without Jesus. I need His anointing and I won't let the devil have it. I will commit to having Jesus in me and make no room for the enemy.

This is one of the reasons why I haven't shared my body with another man. I don't want to invite *just* any man's spirit to join with mine. Forming unhealthy soul ties is frightening. My desires are to keep the Holy Spirit and not lose the very presence of God in my life because of pre-marital sexual acts. Yes, I understand that through repentance, the Lord will forgive me for my sinful ways; however, I don't want to risk the special relationship that I have with Jesus. *Be blessed and do what God has purposed (James 1:22, 25).*

Regardless of the sin, I don't want to test God. Having the Lord bless me is essential. I don't want to ruin any treasured gift that the Lord has given me. The man in Proverbs was a victim; however, he had a choice to take another direction and flee from the evil woman rather than stay on her path. He stood there while she spoke to him. Like Eve, he entertained the enemy!

Do you know what makes you feel vulnerable or what your temptations are? It's a good idea to discover where your weaknesses are. Pray about those weak places in your life.

Ask the Lord to help you in that area because the enemy knows what they are too. Anyone can become tempted in some form or another but the Word of God is powerful. This is how the enemy is defeated. Keep the Word in your heart so that you will not sin against God. (*Psalms 119:11*)

Having the Spirit of God is essential for us to resist temptation. We also need to be equipped with the Word to make us strong during our weak moments. (*II Timothy 3:16, 17*) "*Equip yourself with the word.*" When you feel the temptation coming upon you say, "*Get behind Me, Satan!*" *Mark 8:31* What's so important about this scripture was that Jesus spoke the Word back to the devil. God's words will strengthen you and make you strong in temptation.

II Timothy 3:16
"*All Scripture is given by inspiration of God, and is profitable for doctrine, for reproof, for correction, for instruction in righteousness, that the man of God my be complete, thoroughly equipped for every good work.*"

When you feel like you are being tempted quote this scripture, 1 John 4:4:

"*He that is in* _____ *is stronger than he*
that is in the world."
(Place your name here)

Be Aware of Counterfeits

Stay filled with the Holy Spirit, stay close to the Lord and stay in His word. Watch out for counterfeits.

I Corinthians 2:9-16
"*Eye has not seen, nor ear heard,*
Nor have entered into the heart of man

*the things which God has prepared for those
who love Him."*

*But God has revealed them to us through His Spirit.
For the Spirit searches all things, yes, the deep things
of God.
For what man knows the things of a man except the spirit of
the man which is in him?
Even so no one knows the things of God except
the Spirit of God.
Now we have received, not the spirit of the world, but the
Spirit who is of God, that we might know the things that
have been freely given to us by God.
These things we also speak, not in words which man's
wisdom teaches but which the Holy Spirit teaches,
comparing spiritual things with spiritual.
But the natural man does not receive the things of the Spirit
of God, for they are foolishness to him; nor can he know
them, because they are spiritually discerned.
But he who is spiritual judges all things, yet he himself is
rightly judged by no one.
For "who has known the mind of the Lord that he may
instruct Him?" But we have the mind of Christ.*

Consider all those things you believe you can handle.

*Jeremiah 17: 9
The heart is deceitful above all things*
And desperately wicked;
Who can know it?

Years ago I was attracted to someone who appeared to
have it all together. He was polite, charming and very attractive. He was also involved with drug activities, constantly
lied and he begged for money. For weeks, I tried to overlook

his faults because I enjoyed his company. I became involved in things that weren't of God. Foolishly, I continued to date him for a few weeks, pretending that his lifestyle was okay. It suddenly became clear to me that he was on a path of destruction and I was going right along with him if I continued to date him. I ended the relationship abruptly. The truth is, this man was a liar, a cheat and a counterfeit. Because I entertained him for so long, I almost got caught up.

Jeremiah 17:5-6
Thus says the Lord:
Cursed is the man who trusts in man
And makes flesh his strength,
Whose heart departs from the Lord.
For he shall be like a shrub in the desert,
And shall not see when good comes,
But shall inhabit the parched places in the wilderness,
In a salt land which is not inhabited.

I pray you never meet a counterfeit. A counterfeit is designed to destroy every good thing about you.

James 1:16-18
Don't be deceived, my beloved brethren.
Every good and perfect gift is from above, coming down from the Father of the lights, with whom there is no variation or shadow of turning.

Don't be fooled by counterfeits. He may be a sweet young man in Church, handsome, wealthy, charming, and educated. Then one day you realize that the new gentleman in your life has a drug addiction or sells drugs or he may be trying to entice you into doing things that you know are wrong. You are on a mission! Don't fall for it. That particular mate is not from God. Be patient. Wait for the Lord to move and bless you with a good man.

Ask the Lord to show you His will for your life. Pray when a new boyfriend or acquaintance enters the picture. Ask the Lord if the new man means to harm or hinder you in any way. Be aware and be careful, especially if you are of the age to date. Ask for the Lord's presence and guidance in all you do. Remember counterfeits are tricks and traps to take you off of your path of righteousness. Counterfeits can also come in any package.

Galatians 6:16-26
I say then: Walk in the Spirit, and you shall not fulfill
the lust of the flesh.
For the flesh lusts against the Spirit, and the Spirit against
the flesh; and these are contrary to one another, so that you
do not do the things that you wish.

But if you are led by the Spirit, you are not under the law.
Now the works of the flesh are evident, which are: adul-
tery, fornication uncleanness, lewdness, idolatry, sorcery,
hatred, contentions, jealousies, outbursts of wrath, selfish
ambitions, dissensions, heresies, envy, murders, drunken-
ness, revelries, and the like; of which I tell you beforehand,
just as I also told you in time past, that those who practice
such things will not inherit the kingdom of God.

But the fruit of the Spirit is love, joy, peace, longsuffering,
kindness, goodness, faithfulness, gentleness, self-control.
Against such there is no law.
And those who are Christ's have crucified the flesh with its
passions and desires.
If we live in the Spirit, let us also walk in the Spirit.
Let us not become conceited, provoking one another,
envying one another.

Prayer

Give me the wisdom, Lord Jesus, so that I may determine what is meant for good and what is meant for evil in my life.

I need your help, O Lord.

Protect my thoughts.

Fill my mind with thoughts of you so that I may not have much room for evil thoughts and evil ways.

Help me to walk in the Spirit and to avoid paths of destruction.

Show me when I sin against you. Teach me how to repent.

Help me to be obedient to Your Word

In Jesus' Name.

CHAPTER 9

Question: 9
Should I Date Guys Who Don't Believe In Abstinence?

DATING

II Corinthians 6:14
Do not be unequally yoked together with unbelievers.
For what fellowship has righteousness with lawlessness?
And what communion has light with darkness?
And what accord has Christ with Belial?
Or what part has a believer with an unbeliever?
And what agreement has the temple of God with idols?
For you are the temple of the living God. As God has said:
Therefore
Come out from among them
And be separate, says the Lord.
Do not touch what is unclean,
And I will receive you. I will be a Father to you,
And you shall be My sons and daughters,
Says the Lord Almighty.

Dating simply means to go out socially. A date can be referred to as a companion. I pray that you make good decisions regarding dating and the company you keep.

Proverbs 13:20
He who walks with wise men will be wise,
But the companion of fools will be destroyed.

Dating can be an exciting part of your young adult life. Dating is a way of learning others' personalities, likes, habits, and interests that may be similar to your own. Dating is especially exciting when you fellowship with people of similar ages, interests, and faith. Dating can be rather difficult, however.

Dating Difficulties

Now for the question that I have been asked hundreds of times, does a person who is celibate date? The answer is, some date, some don't. Some people may find dating enjoyable and they like to socialize. However, I must say that some people living their life for the Lord, will find dating discouraging, frustrating, and difficult.

Difficulties come when the one you date doesn't share the same beliefs as you do. Things may be fine in the beginning of the friendship. However, I know from my own experience, that problems arise when the one you are dating wants more from the relationship than you do. The above scriptures states,

Do not be unequally yoked together with unbelievers.

I happen to agree with this scripture. I also believe in trusting the Lord in my relationships. I believe in praying before accepting a date, before the date, and even during the date. Not to come off as super spiritual but I must be real here. Dating is fun but it can lead you to extremely dangerous territory when you are committed to live your life for the Lord. Living the lifestyle of celibacy may cause men to look in the other direction; however, being celibate is an excellent way to weed out the men who are just looking for a sexual relationship.

Dating Determination

First you have to determine if dating is for you. Some of you may not be at an age where dating is appropriate for you. Second, if you aren't a mature person, perhaps dating will be a little overwhelming. Thirdly, if it's not in your faith to date others prior to marriage, than don't. If the Lord is dealing with you, regarding dating, then obey God. One thing you should remember is that if you aren't ready to date, don't. If you feel uncomfortable being alone with an individual, go with a group of friends or don't go at all. If you feel that your flesh is weak and you are tempted to be intimate with your date, please don't go alone. Try not to be alone with your date.

Dating Dilemmas

Unfortunately, people usually put certain standards on dating such as expecting physical involvement and/or sexual contact. Going out on a date should be about socialization. No one should feel any pressure to do things they feel aren't right or do things they aren't ready to do.

Personally, I enjoyed dating. I had more friendly relationships than love relationships. The men I dated were more like big brothers than boyfriends. All my life I believed that the Lord would provide the right mate for me. I figured that the right man would come along and that the Lord would love me through that mate. Unfortunately, as I got older I was impatient and made some wrong choices for myself while dating. I learned the hard way and experienced heartaches and headaches through immature relationships.

Psalms 1:1
Blessed is the man
Who walks not in the counsel of the ungodly,
Nor stands in the path of sinners,

Those bad choices I made in relationships helped develop the person I am today, however. I asked the Lord to help me with all my life's decisions. In dating, we should still be concerned about pleasing God with our walk and our talk. Getting emotionally attached to someone in a relationship that is not of God can cause you a lot of heartache and pain not to mention pressure and stress. Perhaps the person you want to be with does not believe in waiting for marriage. What will you do then? A relationship not of God is a dangerous one for a young Christian. In dating, I believe that the two should have the same faith in Christ and especially the same views on waiting to experience sex.

Amos 3:3
Can two walk together, unless they are agreed?

You can ask the Lord for a saved companion. The Lord answered my prayers years ago by providing a good man in my life. I had asked for a God-fearing, funny, charming, attractive, independent, hard working, patient man. I actually got more than I asked for. The Lord blessed me with a friend and a companion; however, I had to be careful not to cross the lines of our relationship.

When the Lord sent this man in my life, I knew it was for friendship only. This man was my covering, for three years. This man wasn't totally receptive of my lifestyle; however, he did support me and protect me from unnecessary stresses. This man wasn't the "husband" the Lord had for me. The Lord used this man to be my covering and I was loved and protected by God through him. When things became complicated, I asked the Lord to end the relationship. I felt that our friendship was becoming a hindrance to the things God had planned for me. He did end the relationship!

People always ask me about dating while being celibate. Many want to know, "How do you date and not become physically involved?" If you are currently in a relationship or if you are dating and you want to live your life for the Lord, here a few ways to live a lifestyle worth celebrating.

DATING TIPS

1) Ask yourself this:
Who do you walk with? (*Amos 3:3*. Does my date believe in the same things that I do?
Do we agree?

Psalm 1:1 "Blessed is the man who walks not in the counsel of the ungodly..."

We tend to take on the attitudes and beliefs of those we date.

I Corinthians 15:33-34
"Do not be deceived: Evil company corrupts good habits, Awake to righteousness, and do not sin;..."

2) Ask yourself this: Am I carnal minded?
Am I concerned about pleasing the Lord or this man?
Am I lusting after my date?

Romans 8:5-6

*For those who live according to the flesh set their minds on
the things of the flesh, but those who live according to the
Spirit, the things of the Spirit.
For to be carnally minded is death, but to be spiritually
minded is life and peace.*

When I felt the desire to participate in sexual activities
while dating, I felt as if I were disappointing Jesus. I felt as
if I were being rebellious and disobedient. I couldn't deny
Jesus. I knew that I couldn't please the Lord while being in
the flesh.

*Romans 8:8
So then, those who are in the flesh cannot please God*

3) Always state what you believe in. Tell that boyfriend,
date, or companion about the goals you have set for your
life. If the person you're involved with cares for you, he will
also care for the things that make you happy and about the
things that are important to you. You must be careful with
your heart and consider who you give it to.

*Proverbs 4:23
Keep your heart with all diligence,
For out of it spring the issues of life.*

Watch your heart. Give your heart to the Lord. Ask Him
to protect it. Take your dating relationship to the Lord. Trust
that He will lead you and guide you in the right way.

4) Remember that you belong to God. You are His. You were
bought with a price. His blood has covered you. We serve
a jealous God. Naturally, you have experienced a jealous
feeling before. I must explain that jealousy is different from
envy. Envy can be defined as desiring something that belongs

to someone else. An example would the desire of a sports car, a great job or a new home. Jealousy can be defined as demanding exclusive loyalty. We belong to God. God is a jealous God. No one should put anything or anyone before God. God should be number one, first in your life. Remember what God told those who worshipped false gods.

Deuteronomy 5:9
"You shall not bow down to them nor serve them.
For I, the Lord your God, am a jealous God,..."

Jealousy is the result of you putting that something or someone before the Lord. Don't worship a man so much that you begin to miss Church services or you fail to pray like you used to. When you start to dedicate yourself to a man and you are not given to him in marriage, it is unacceptable to the Lord.

The Lord is my husband. Why would I put another man before Him?

Matthew 6:24
No man can serve two masters: for either he will hate the one and love the other, or else he will be loyal to the one and despise the other.
You cannot serve God and mammon.

5) Always Represent! If you are going to date, you must remember to be modest, humble, and pure in heart, mind, and spirit. Remember you are a princess representing the kingdom of God. Your clothes, attitude, and your character should reflect that.

I Peter 3:3

135

*Do not let your adornment be merely outward—
arranging the hair, wearing gold, or putting
on fine apparel-
Rather let it be the hidden person of the heart, with
the incorruptible beauty of a gentle and quiet spirit,
which is very precious in the sight of God.*

In our walk of celibacy, we are worshipping the Father in our walk and our talk. Show your good nature. Show Jesus instead of showing off.

*I Timothy 2:9
"...in like manner also, that the women adorn themselves
in modest apparel, with propriety and moderation, not with
braided hair or gold or pearls or costly clothing, but, which
is proper for women professing godliness,
with good works."*

6) Don't be anxious. Be patient! If you feel lonely and desire a companion, by all means, don't go looking for someone to date. Also try not to look at what other people are doing in their relationships, look at God and wait for Him to reveal your destiny.

7) Be ye sanctified!

*I Peter 2:11 "Beloved, I beg you as sojourners and
pilgrims, abstain from fleshly lusts which war against the
soul, having your conduct honorable...."*

*I Thessalonians 4:3
For this is the will of God, your sanctification: that you
should abstain from sexual immorality; that each of you
should know how to possess his own vessel in sanctification
and honor, not in passion of lust, like the Gentiles*

who do not know God;

4:7-8
For God did not call us to uncleanness, but to holiness.
Therefore he who rejects this does not reject man, but God,
who has also given us His Holy Spirit.

8) Don't indulge in sinful acts. Consider your ways. Consider your consequences. If you are not sexually active yet, don't start.

Song of Solomon 8:4
"I charge you, O daughters of Jerusalem,
Do not stir up nor awaken love
Until it pleases."

Don't allow your behavior or the behavior of your date to ignite sexual feelings and desires. Once you start, it is difficult to stop and control your actions and the actions of your date.

Ecclesiastes 10: 8-9
"He who digs a pit will fall into it,
And whoever breaks through a wall will be bitten
by a serpent.
He who quarries stones may be hurt by them,
And he who splits wood may be endangered by it."

9) Put off the "old" you. The way you used to date and interact with others should change from your new walk with Christ. You are a new creature. You are now set apart from others to worship the Lord. You can't participate in any former sinful ways and habits. You are renewed.

Ephesians 4:22-24
"..put off, concerning your former conduct, the old man
which grows corrupt according to the deceitful lust,
and be renewed in the spirit of your mind,
and that you put on the new man which was created
according to God, in true righteousness and holiness."

10) Be strong in the Lord. When you date, put on your spiritual clothing.

Ephesians 6:10-11
Finally, my brethren, be strong in the Lord and in the
power of His might.
Put on the whole armor of God, that you may be able to
stand against the wiles of the devil.

6:13-17
Therefore take up the whole armor of God, that you
may be able to withstand in the evil day,
and having done all, to stand.
Stand therefore, having girded your waist with truth,
having put on the breastplate of righteousness, and
having shod your feet with the preparation
of the gospel of peace;
Above all, taking the shield of faith with which you will
be able to quench all the fiery darts of the wicked one.
And take the helmet of salvation,
and the sword of the Spirit, which is the word of God;

11) Let the Holy Spirit teach you when dating. We can't depend on our flesh or our natural mind to discern spiritual things. We need the Spirit of God to teach us spiritual things. Therefore in choosing to date or even finding friends to hang out with, invite the Holy Spirit to assist you with your decision.

I Corinthian 2:12-14
Now we have received, not the spirit of the world, but
the Spirit who is from God, that we might know the
things that have been freely given to us by God.
These things we also speak, not in words which man's
wisdom teaches but which the Holy Spirit teaches,
comparing spiritual things with spiritual.

Romans 8:16
The Spirit Himself bears witness with our spirit that we are
children of God.

12) Be sober. Having a sober mind is a necessity when dating. You must have a clear mind regarding what you will and will not stand for. The word sober has several meanings. It means not being intoxicated, but being serious, solemn, or sedate. One who is sober is one who has their sanity and/or self-control.

I Peter 5:8
Be sober, be vigilant; because your adversary
the devil
walks about like a roaring lion, seeking whom
he may devour.

One needs to be sober in their mind, serious, and aware of what they are doing at all times. Being sober is realizing who you are and not being double-minded. Be serious for what you stand for and for what you believe. Don't let your actions led you to destruction. Be of the right mind (rational) when you go out. God is not the author of confusion. Realize that the devil uses tricks to discourage, upset and confuse you so that you are unable to make good decisions.

13) Pray before you accept the date. Pray before the date. Pray during the date and pray after. Be honest with Jesus. Tell Him about your pain, desires, problems and concerns. Dating while living a life of celibacy produces many challenges. You will be faced with tests, trials and temptations. Remember that living a life of celibacy has many rewards. You must persevere. Dating does not have to be about sex. Remember this scripture for encouragement.

"Blessed is the man who
perseveres under trial, because when he has stood the test,
he will receive the crown of life that
God has promised to those who love him."
James 1:12

14) Know the Word of God and keep it hidden in your heart. For many will try to deceive you!

Colossians 2:4
Now this I say lest anyone should deceive you with
persuasive words.

2:8-10
Beware lest anyone cheat you through philosophy and
empty deceit, according to the tradition of men, according
to the basic principles of the world, and not according
to Christ.
For in Him dwells all the fullness of the Godhead bodily;
and you are complete in Him, who is the head of all
principality and power.

Don't be deceived. Don't you fall for it! You are complete in Christ and no one can take that away.

15) Write the vision. Write down your decision to keep yourself celibate. Write your plans and set goals for what you will and will not do. Remember, what type of man you are looking for. Do you want the one who will pressure you or the one who treasures you? If the man is not living up to your standards, go home! Never compromise! Don't give in, and don't settle. Never reduce your standards, princess. You can make it!

16) Don't look for a man. Allow the Lord to bring your prince to you. Most of all be patient and realize that:

"...No good thing will He withhold from those who walk uprightly." (Psalms 84:11).

17) Be a good steward.
Be a good steward of all that the Lord has given you, especially your body.
You are a vessel, a home, and a dwelling place for the Lord's Spirit. Be a good steward of the Lord's home.

Romans 12:1
...present your bodies a living sacrifice, holy, acceptable unto God, which is your reasonable service.

The Lord told me one day to take care of His house and that He would take care of mine. I knew that the Lord wanted me to keep my house, His house. The Lord dwells in me.

I Corinthians 3:16
Do you not know that you are the temple of God and that the Spirit of God dwells in you?

I am a dwelling place for Jesus. I need to make sure that I keep my house free from all impurities, free from alcohol, free from drugs and free from *soul ties* with others. I need to take care of my house. God gave me this house. God provided everything I need in this house; therefore, there is no need for the alcohol, drugs and sex. I am a host for the Holy Spirit, the Lord dwells within me.

I Corinthians 6:19-20
Or do you not know that your body is the temple of the
Holy Spirit who is in you, whom you have from God, and
you are not your own.
For you were bought at a price; therefore glorify God in
your body and in your spirit, which are God's.

I am a vessel for the Lord. I'm determined to be a good and faithful steward.

18) Think on Him! When you stay focused, you keep your mine stayed on Him!

Philippians 4:8
Finally, brethren, whatever things are true, whatever things
are noble, whatever things are just, whatever things are
pure, whatever things are lovely, whatever things are of
good report, if there is any virtue and if there is anything
praiseworthy-meditate on these things.

Romans 12: 2
And do not be conformed to this world,
but be transformed by the renewing of your mind,
that you may prove what is
that good and acceptable
and
perfect will of God.

19) Let the Lord be the judge, the ruler, and the final answer. Let the Lord be your referee, the umpire and the commissioner. Make it His call. You must be honest with the Lord and pray about your weaknesses so that He can assist you while dating. *"And let the peace of Christ rule in your heart" (Colossians 3:15).*

Flesh is weak! We need to admit our weakness and seek the Lord's help.

Romans7: 19-24
For the good that I will to do, I do not do; but the evil I will not to do, that I practice.
Now if I do what I will not to do, it is no longer I who do it, but sin that dwells in me.
I find then a law, that evil is present with me, the one who wills to do good.

For I delight in the law of God according to the inward man.
But I see another law in my members warring against the law of my mind, and bringing me into captivity to the law of sin, which is in my members.
O wretched man that I am! Who will deliver me from this body of death?

In this scripture, Paul referred to his body of flesh as the body of this death. Our flesh wrestles against the spirits of the world (carnality) and with the spirit of the Lord. The enemy knows your weaknesses. Try not to get caught up by the sweet talkers, those charmers telling you everything you want to hear. Those charmers will tell you that you are beautiful, wonderful, and intelligent. You already know that because the Word says so.

Allow the Lord to reveal to you what He desires of your life. Remember the Lord knows your thoughts and knows your dates' thoughts and motives. Give the Lord your concerns and ask Him for His guidance. His call is the best call! Follow His rules and be blessed, for the Lord says,

Jeremiah 29:11
For I know the thoughts that I think toward you, says the
Lord, thoughts of peace and not of evil, to give you
a future and a hope.

20) Pray that the Lord will keep you in the hour of temptation.

Matthew 6:13
And do not lead us into temptation but deliver us
from the evil one.

Temptation means solicit to sin. I can tell you from experience that dating someone and trying to live your life for the Lord is difficult. One has to be strong mentally, emotionally, and spiritually. After all, it's our human nature to have sexual feelings and desires. This is why it's essential to pray about the relationship so that you won't fall into temptation.

James 1:12
Blessed is the man who endures temptation, for when he
has been approved, he will receive the crown of life
which the Lord has promised to those who love Him.

James 1:13
Let no one say when he is tempted, "I am tempted by God";
for God cannot be tempted by evil, nor does He
Himself tempt anyone.
But each one is tempted when he is drawn away by his own
desires and enticed.

*Then, when desire has conceived, it gives birth to sin; and
sin, when it is fullgrown, brings forth death.*

Temptation will be the hardest challenge for you in
dating. One of the main reasons is because many will fall
under the influence of those they date. Prayer is needed when
you date so that you can resist the solicitation to sin and be
able to not believe or receive any negative influences that are
not of God.

The power of influence!

Reflection Story

We live in a spiritual world. Philosophical and intellectual experiences can influence one greatly, especially those in college. A strong Christian, a firm and long-time believer of Christ may be sitting in a lecture hall under the influence of a professor who is a profound atheist. This isn't a rare case in colleges and universities. I had my own experience with a professor who claimed to be an atheist. He was always talking about his lack of faith and his disapproval of what Christians do.

After listening to the professor for several classes mentioning his beliefs, I didn't think it was going to bother me. He was certainly entitled to his own thoughts just as long as he didn't cause me to participate in things I didn't believe in. Surely I would speak up if he caused me to take part in blasphemous things, right?

Around Easter that year I sat in a lecture hall with about 200 students. The professor tried to compare Christians who celebrated Easter, to a cult named Heaven's Gate. This cult followed the direction of their leader, M.H. Applewhite. The cult followed this leader to their very deaths. They believed that a spaceship was trailing the Hale-Bopp comet, and all of them committed suicide by eating poison in hopes to fly away with the imaginary spaceship. It was a shocking and disturbing story. Why the comparison of these two events? Was the professor crazy? Someone had to correct him. He was totally out of line. How could anyone let him get away with that sick, distorted analogy?

I was reeling after hearing the professor's statement; however, what about the other 199 students in the same class? Surely one of my fellow classmates believed in Christ and surely at least one of them has celebrated Easter? Why isn't anyone standing up for his or her beliefs.... for Jesus, I thought? I did the unthinkable. Myself, forever known as being quiet and shy, challenged the professor. The professor was outraged. I have never seen anyone become so sweaty and red that quickly. Perhaps no one has ever considered questioning this professor's opinion in class. But, I did!

You see, I simply knew better. I knew Jesus and I knew that you couldn't compare Jesus to some cult that convinces people to commit suicide. First of all, the Bible teaches us that we are not are own. Yes, we have free will but we are not to take our own life or anyone else's. This teacher lashed out at me but I stood firm. I couldn't believe what he was saying. He tried to out talk me so I remained calm and decided not to give in to an argument. I wanted him to know that not everyone believed his ideas let alone agree with him. The Lord gave me the confidence to speak and the peace to remain calm. The Lord knew that His people whether they stood for Him or not, weren't to hear those lies in that class-room. The professor was a nonbeliever and his influence was incredibly powerful because of his position and title. However, with my foundation of Christ, and the help of His Spirit, I had the courage to speak directly to the professor's lie and bring forth the Word, which is the Truth!

I knew back then and I know now, that the *"devil is a liar."* The devil is the master of deceit. He will forever distort the truth. He is constantly trying to destroy the minds of the people of God. The devil is also the master of seduction. Regardless of your purity or your beliefs, your walk of celibacy can become more difficult because of seducing spirits. The longer you are around someone with evil intentions, the more likely you will become more like them. That influential friend or date could eventually lead you to become promiscuous, carnal minded, hooked on drugs, alcohol, and/or spiritually hooked or soul-tied because of their influence.

So, again I question you, *who do you walk with? Tell me, do you know the Word?*

Even the wisest people become greatly influenced by seducing spirits. King Solomon was known for his great wisdom *(1 Kings 1:1-3)*. However, he too was influenced negatively by idol worshipping women. He was influenced so much that he also began to worship false gods.

Dating is a serious decision. Are you able to resist temptation and powerful influences? I strongly suggest that you stay in the Word of God on a daily basis. Put on the full Armor of God, walk in the Spirit of God, and stand on His strength. When you date, ask the Lord if that person is there to help or hinder you. Ask the Lord to show you why that person is in your life. The Lord will reveal this to you.

Continue to pray so that you will not fall into temptation, for the reward you obtain from waiting is far greater than any temporary thrill. If you do make the decision to date, always remember to put God first in all that you do!

Prayer

Lord, it is my desire to please you in my walk and my talk.
Help me to honor you in all my ways.

I ask that you will keep my mind, my heart, and my body.
In dating, I pray that you will show me if he (my date) is
here to hinder me in any way from You.
I ask that you will give me the type of love you want me to
have for this man.
Show me why he is in my life.

Give me the wisdom to make good decisions.
Give me the strength to keep your Word and to stay
on the path of righteousness.

PART III

How Can I Be Close To God When All I Do Is Sin?

CHAPTER 10

Question 10:
How Can I Possibly Forgive
Someone Who Has Hurt Me?

FORGIVENESS
The love of God covers a multitude of sins!

We have all made mistakes and poor decisions in our lives. Thankfully, we have people who are willing to forgive us and teach us how powerful forgiveness is. I can remember an early lesson of forgiveness as a child. My mother had poured a glass of milk for me. While eating my breakfast I knocked over the glass of milk and it made a horrible mess. I was so sorry for my mistake that I burst into tears. My mother ran over to me and calmed me down. She grabbed a mop to clean and told me a story about one of my favorite uncles. Apparently, he was a little clumsy and would spill his milk numerous times even as an adult! Because I adored my uncle so much, I felt better to know that he too made mistakes. My mother's act of forgiveness and kindness taught me so much. I think about it often still when I drop things.

There are times when people offend far worst than spilled milk. They intentions are to hurt. How can we find it in our hearts to forgive someone who has caused us pain? Consider Jesus' act of forgiveness. The very ones He loved and prayed for denied him. The same ones he healed and helped, yelled out "crucify him!" They murdered Jesus. Yet Jesus prayed for them to be forgiven.

Forgiveness is a necessity for our lives. It's God's will that we forgive others as He forgives us. When we don't forgive others, we sin. Also, when we sin and fail to ask God for forgiveness (repent), we separate ourselves from God.

Israel 59:2
But your iniquities have separated you from your God;
And your sins have hidden His face from you,
So that He will not hear

Repenting is essential for all of us especially if you are aware of the goodness of God and all that He has done for us.

Romans 2:4
"Or do you despise the riches of His goodness, forbearance, and longsuffering, not knowing that the goodness of God leads you to repentance?"

I John 1:9
"If we confess our sins, He is faithful and just to forgive us our sins and to cleanse us from all unrighteousness."

Imagine making footprints in sand. Those imprints you once left behind will be washed away by the ocean and will never reappear. Your past steps (sins) can be washed away by the Lord. You can have a new slate all over again when you repent. Those experiences of your past can't be relived, can't be revisited, and will not happen again. The only thing that may be repeated is another sinful act. In this walk of celibacy, you must ask for forgiveness and live your life to please the Lord.

Personally, I have made plenty of mistakes. No one is perfect. I knew I needed forgiveness for my past mistakes. If you have already participated in sexual intercourse with someone and you wish you had waited, repent of the act and ask for forgiveness. It's also important that you forgive yourself as well. Ask the Lord to help deliver you from your acts of sin. You should also pray that the Lord would keep you for the right man in marriage. God is the only one who can forgive you of all things, restore you, and give you back your dignity and self-respect. Nobody but God can release you from whatever situation you are in.

We'll pray:

Psalms 51:2
Wash me thoroughly from my iniquity,
And cleanse me from my sin

God will answer:

Jeremiah 31:34
"For I will forgive their iniquity, and their sin I will
remember no more."

God sends His Word, heals us, and delivers us from destruction. If you desire forgiveness, ask God for it and forgive yourself. Desire a change in your life and recognize the importance of repentance.

Please don't allow yourself to believe the lies of this world, saying that God doesn't love you. God loves you perfectly. Your sins may be keeping you away from the presence of God; however, He would love to have you closer to Him. He desires for you to turn away from your sin.

Isaiah 59:2
But your iniquities have separated you from you God;
And your sins have hidden His face from you,
So that He will not hear.
Ephesians 4:30
"And do not grieve the Holy Spirit of God, by whom you
were sealed for the day of redemption. Let all bitterness,
and wrath, and anger and clamor, and evil speaking be put
away from you with all malice. And be kind to one another,
tenderhearted, forgiving one another,
even as God in Christ forgave you."
I John 1:9

Jesus gave the ultimate sacrifice, His very life. Some of us fail to sacrifice temporary pleasures for the Lord. Your walk of celibacy requires sacrifice. We may fail at obedience, however; we can still remain close to the Lord through repentance and forgiveness.

Acts 2:38, 40
"...Repent, and let every one of you be baptized in this
name of Jesus Christ for the remission of sins; and you
shall receive the gift of the Holy Spirit."

"...Be saved from this perverse generation."

Asking for forgiveness as well as forgiving others is essential.

The Unforgiving

Did you know that when you don't forgive those who have wronged you, that you also give them permission to control you. They continue to control your mind, actions, emotions, and your spirit. There have been people who really hurt me and I was hurt even more by continually playing back their ill treatment in my mind. One particular lady, I will call "Eva" made my life unbearable.

She literally ruled me everyday because of all the control I gave to her. I allowed myself to think of her night and day. Each person I would talk to, I would somehow find a way to enter her into the conversation. One day the Lord showed me that I needed to forgive her and move on. The Lord also told me to no longer discuss her or dwell on her wrong doings. This was the answer I needed. Believe it or not, she was hard to let go. Even after she hurt me and mistreated me, you would think that I was happy to let her go, but I wasn't.

I continued to discuss her until one day my anger turned to tears. After weeks of dealing with my pain, I broke down and cried about the pain. She wasn't a bad person but a hurting person. Therefore, I was able to see why she mistreated me and was finally able to release her to the Lord and let go of my pain. What a relief.

Even if I wasn't able to figure out her ill treatment of me, I am sure I would have been able to release her to the Lord with His help. My tears came because I realized how much I cared for her in the first place. It was simply time to go our separate ways and the parting wasn't what I had ever anticipated. However, it was necessary for my own good, growth, and maturation. I needed to learn forgiveness in order to appreciate being forgiven.

So how does one forgive? Seek the Lord's help in forgiveness. Learn how to forgive automatically. If someone hit you, stole from you or lied to you, forgive them and their awful they behavior. Many times people believe that forgiveness gives permission for that person to do more terrible things to you. This is not so. Forgive them and don't allow the mistreatment to continue.

Releasing that person is the key. Give them over to God. Say, "God, I give you so and so, because I can't hold on to the pain she caused me." Then pray for that individual. The Lord showed me how to love my enemies. I had to like them on their good days and love them on their bad. Understand that their bad days were the days in which they required much prayer. This is when the enemy operated in them the most. They were going through their own misery therefore causing others to suffer around them. The Lord desires for us to pray for their hurts, their pain, and their ways. Pray for peace in their life. Remember that when you bless them, you will be blessed.

Acknowledge the sin you did. Think about how you may have provoked the behavior. I must say that there have been more than a few occasions when I was mistreated, and I clearly didn't provoke the behavior. However, I did research the possibility of how I could have hurt that individual in any way. Pray and ask God to reveal any pain you may have caused.

The enemy wants to distract you on your journey to your divine purpose. Don't allow any negative thoughts to linger in your mind. There is too much written in the Word for you not to know the truth about who you are. You are a child of God. You are fearfully and wonderfully made (*Psalms 139*).

Nothing is impossible for God. If you have sinned and you are dealing with feelings of regret and shame, repent. Turn away from the sin and the Lord will forgive you. Don't allow the devil to torment you with the thoughts of your past failures and past mistakes.

The enemy wants to tear you down, lie to you, and make you feel dirty, ashamed, and defeated. The Lord will forgive, renew, rebuild, sanctify, and cleanse you.

It is essential for you to acknowledge the sin, ask the Lord to break the hold that the world has on you (bondage) for the sin has become habitual (Sexual relations, pornography, soul ties). You can start anew.

Create in me a new thing
Ephesians 4:23
"...and be renewed in the Spirit of your mind, and that you put on the new man which was created according to God, in true righteousness and holiness."

Prayer

Lord, I come before You with thanksgiving.

*I praise You for keeping me in my right mind.
Strengthen, every weak area, Lord.*

*Teach me how to forgive those who have hurt me. Teach me
how to release them to you Lord.*

*Purge, Lord, where my faults lie. Create in me a clean
heart.
Keep my mind, Lord, so that I may continue my focus on
the things of God.
Lead and direct me Lord. Place my feet on the right paths.*

*Remind me of the purpose You have for my life so that I
may continue to walk upright.*

*Crown me, Lord Jesus, with righteousness.
Deliver me from the enemy who wishes to war against me.
Make me strong in Your name. Redeem me, Lord.*

Amen

CHAPTER 11

Question 11:
Why Do I Continue To Repeat the Sin After Repenting of It?

Deliverance
Breaking the Yoke of Sin

Galatians 5:1
Stand fast therefore in the liberty,
by which Christ has made us free,
and do not be entangled again with a yoke of bondage.

So many people have asked how to break the cycle of sin. The only answer I have is deliverance. Deliverance means to set free or to make good. Deliverance brings liberation and freedom. Sin leads to more sin and sin leads to bondage. Be set free from the bondage of sin. With the help of Jesus you can become delivered, set free from sin and its hold on your life.

In order to receive deliverance, you must want deliverance. If you don't seek deliverance you will stay in the situation you are in. Sin is like a cancerous growth destroying and causing damage to all that is good about you. Sin separates us from the Lord.

Romans 6:16
"Do you not know that to whom you present yourselves slaves to obey, you are that one's slaves whom you obey. Whether of sin leading to death, or of obedience leading to righteousness?"

In order to be successful in your walk of celibacy, you have to want deliverance from anything that is not of God. The problem with being involved with men in an intimate or sexual way is that we tend to form addictions, compulsive behaviors, and soul-ties. We become oppressed and suffer from bondage.

The Lord can help you live the type of life that is pleasing to Him. You have to be willing, however, to close any gate that may give the devil entry and access to you.

1 John 3:8
"He who sins is of the devil, for the devil has sinned from the beginning. For this purpose the Son of God was manifested, that He might destroy the works of the devil."

Steps toward deliverance:

1) Forgiveness is key. You must repent of all sin. The longer you hang on to your sinful ways or try to hide your sin, the longer you are in bondage to the sin. Confess all of your sinful ways to the Lord. Don't leave out anything. Be honest with Jesus. The sooner you confess them, the better.

Proverbs 28:13
"He who covers his sins will not prosper,
But whoever confesses and forsakes them will have mercy."

Tell the Lord what you need help with and repent of all of your sinful actions. It's essential to acknowledge all sins. You already know what things are not of God.

Psalms 32:3-5
When I kept silent, my bones grew old
Through my groaning all the day long.
For day and night Your hand was heavy upon me;
My vitality was turned into the drought of summer. Selah
I acknowledge my sin to You, and my iniquity
I have not hidden.
I said, " I will confess my transgressions to the Lord," and
You forgave the iniquity of my sin. Selah

2) Forgive anyone who has wronged you or hurt you regardless of what the person has done. The Bible says that we must forgive others as Christ forgives us. The longer you hold grudges and are unforgiving, the longer you hinder the blessings of God.

Ephesians 4:32
"And be kind to one another, tenderhearted, forgiving one
another, even as God in Christ forgave you."

3) Desire deliverance. You have to want it! Get rid of any magazines, pornographic movies, and books that may be distracting and damaging to your spirit. End all phone calls, emails and letters or correspondence to that person(s) from whom you need deliverance.

You also have to be willing to separate yourself from any person(s) who have unclean spirits. The more we associate with people with unclean spirits, the more we become like them. In dating, we tend to want to impress our dates. Many of us begin to take on the nature of the men we date. When you ask for deliverance, you have to want to rid yourself of anything that is not of God. This includes those men in your life who have been distracting and damaging to your spirit.

Reflection Story

Deliverance has become a personal story of my very own. After making a vow to remain celibate until marriage, I thought I would never have to deal with soul-ties. However, soul-ties are not only formed by sexual intercourse. You can actually form a soul-tie through the people you are close to in one form or another. My soul-tie was formed through a dating relationship that I had years ago.

This old flame came back into my life via e-mails. In all honesty, I didn't think that my old flame was an issue with my walk with Christ. I never thought those emails were damaging to my spirit but they were. The Lord allowed me to see that I actually found joy in receiving emails from him and responding to him. The problem was that old feelings and desires resurfaced when he would contact me. I began to think about him more and reminisce about the past. This was someone that the Lord delivered me from and yet we were still connected.

After several months I made the decision to end the friendship. I told a close friend of mine to pray for me because I knew the decision to release him would be hard but the process would be even more difficult.

Several months later I was in touch with my old flame again. Then one day, I was working on this book and realized that I had to complete the chapter on deliverance. I took my own advice about deliverance, researched and wrote more about how to obtain it. My prayer then became one of great honesty. I told God all about my situation. I wasn't safe from soul-ties.

Revelation then came that soul-ties can happen to anyone in relationships such as father-son, mother-child, best friends and boyfriend-girlfriends. People even have strong connections or soul-ties to objects and things. After realizing what I was into, I made the best decision ever. I decided to release this friendship entirely. No longer were emails sent and all messages from him were deleted. My deliverance came when I made the effort to be free.

If you have a problem and need deliverance, know that the answer comes when you make the decision to be free. When the Lord delivers you from whatever the situation (drugs/alcohol, debt, diseases, soul-ties) remember that you have to be a good steward of the gift that the Lord gives you. Be a good steward of your deliverance! You are free to do all that God has given you to do. I am free to be a good and faithful woman to my spouse. I am free to honor the Lord. Be set free! Receive and keep your deliverance!

SOUL TIES

What is a soul-tie exactly? A soul-tie is a result of the knitting or tying together of two souls by way of relationships. Relationships such as friendships, father/son, mother/daughter, girlfriend/boyfriend, best friends, lovers and even those former lovers of your past. Not all soul-ties are negative. Relationships like those of Jonathon and David and Ruth and Naomi were relationships of great love and affection. However, many soul-ties, even those of parental relationships, are negative and damaging.

We must understand that adultery and sexual activity is dangerous to the soul. You don't necessarily have to have sexual intercourse to become connected or tied to a person.

However, the more people you share your body with in an intimate way, the more divided your spirit man can be. In addition, your soul is your inner man or inner being or spirit man. Your heart, mind, and emotions represent your soul.

Genesis says that the desire of the woman shall be for her husband or for the mate who becomes her first soul-tied partner or her sexual partner. (Genesis 3:16).

Genesis 2:24
"Therefore a man shall leave his father
and his mother and shall become united and cleave to his
wife, and they shall become one flesh."

The Word of God reinforces how powerful soul-ties are. When two people come together in sexual intercourse they become one flesh. Imagine becoming tied to all of those former lovers and still having their spirits a part of your spirit. Not a pretty thought, huh? So, sexual intercourse builds intimacy. The purpose of this book is to encourage you to wait until marriage and to only share your body with your husband.

A biblical example of a negative soul-tie is Solomon and the connection he shared with his wives. Solomon was a very wise king. However, he was disobedient to God and married women from idol-worshipping nations.

God said:

I Kings 11:2
"You shall not intermarry with them, nor they with you.
Surely they will turn away your hearts after their gods."

Solomon clung to these in love.

These women influenced Solomon greatly. He too began to worship idols. These women cost him greatly. His faith was affected and eventually his kingdom was destroyed after his death.

Another example is found in Genesis. Dinah was the daughter of Jacob and Leah. A man named, Shechem, raped Dinah. After Shechem defiled Dinah, he was soul-tied to her.

Genesis 34:2-3
..he took her and lay with her, and violated her.

167

*His soul was strongly attracted to Dinah
the daughter of Jacob, and
he loved the young woman and spoke kindly to the young
woman.*

Shechem wanted Dinah for his wife. Shechem's father Hamor asked to have Dinah for his son to marry. Hamor spoke to Dinah's father:

Genesis 34:8
*"The soul of my son Shechem longs for your daughter.
Please giver her to him as a wife."*

If you are experiencing a soul-tie and you are feeling the conviction and the holds of it, know that deliverance is an option. The Lord is convicting you because He wants to set you free so that no man, no past partner, no present partner can distract you or take you out of the will of God. Don't let the devil fool you. That relationship you had years ago could have left a spirit inside you, and you must be free from those ties.

Making a conscience step toward your own deliverance is key. You have to want the change! You have to want something better for your life. You have to end all of the lustful urges and longings for those in your past and refocus your attention back to the Lord.

BREAKING THE YOKES

"Do not be unequally yoked together with unbelievers."
II Corinthians 6:14

In order to receive deliverance and maintain it you must separate yourselves from those who don't share your beliefs and goals. Be mindful of the company you keep. If you seek deliverance, why remain with the same crowd that helped you to get into bondage? Cut them loose. Break all ties. Release all of the former friends and acquaintances that aren't of God. I used to see young girls give their lives to God on Sunday and receive His love and then as soon as they left the church, they were back with school friends who didn't share their motivation and determination. The same young girls would be back in church the following Sunday asking for repentance again for their shameful behaviors throughout the week. Perhaps they weren't strong enough to break the ties with their misguided friends. What could have helped these young teens become successful in their walk of righteousness?

Isaiah 10:27 says:
It shall come to pass in that day
That his burden will be taken away from your shoulder,
And his yoke from off your neck,
And the yoke will be destroyed because of the anointing oil.

When you feed on the Word of God, you grow strong, and knowledgeable in things of God. You will become so fat and healthy that you will be able to break and burst apart the yokes that bind you. Building up and strengthening your spirit man with scripture is essential. You will be able to destroy those burdens because of the anointing, the very presence of God in your life.

Having the Lord's anointing on your life will give you total peace. In situations that made you feel defeated, the anointing will cause you to rise up and be triumphant. When the burden of dating, being single or temptation falls upon you, call on the Lord. Let His Spirit rain on you a tremendous blessing that will destroy that heavy burden that is upon you.

Galatians 5:1
Stand fast therefore in the liberty, by
which Christ has made us free,
and do not be entangled again with a yoke of bondage.

He Heals

A friend of mine told me the story of her deliverance. She had contracted genital herpes from a former lover. He was her first lover and he hurt her feelings and her pride. For years she carried the weight of knowing that she was a carrier of this incurable disease.

She met another man, fell in love, slept with him and he then gave her a second form of a sexual transmitted disease. She was devastated. Her pain caused her to be angry but it didn't stop her from being promiscuous. She got another sexually transmitted disease from another man and began to suffer not only emotionally but also physically from pain.

While keeping her diseases secret, she suffered in silence. However, she continued to sleep with men. Finally, she reached out to God for healing. When the Lord told her to stop sleeping with men, she obeyed for a while but she would always go back. Soon, the Lord started to move these men out of her life. Perhaps she wasn't strong enough to sever the ties on her own. She had formed soul-ties with some of these men. As a result, losing these friends devastated her.

Recently, the Lord brought the right man her way. She found herself truly releasing and letting go of her past by seeking deliverance from those soul-ties. She also desired healing. God healed her and asked her to become celibate until marriage. She knew then that her healing came with her obedience and she was responsible for keeping it. She has to be a good steward of her healing and her deliverance. She is now free from all of those diseases and free from her past lovers. A good prayer life and the presence of the Holy

Spirit will keep her and sustain her. The Lord wanted her free and He wanted her obedience. She needs to maintain her blessing and not take any of God's gifts for granted.

If anyone is in Christ, he is a new creation; old things have passed away; behold, all things have become new.
II Corinthians 5:17

Another friend of mine became close friends with a female who was a lesbian. They were good friends and had similar interests. As time went on, my saved, Holy Spirit-filled friend started to become curious about the lifestyle of her new friend. She wondered what sex was like for her, why she desired women and how a same sex relationship possibly fulfilled her. Eventually, my friend found herself wanting to know more. She realized that the spirit that was inside of her friend was powerful and was drawing her in. God revealed to her what she was headed for. She couldn't believe where her interests were leading her. Finally, she broke off the friendship.

That spirit in her new best friend was too strong for her and she realized that she could potentially become more like her friend as opposed to her friend becoming more like Christ. She prayed for her friend's deliverance and for her very own.

Isaiah 43: 18-19
Do not remember the former things,
nor consider the things of old.
Behold, I will do a new thing, now it shall spring forth;
shall you not know it?
I will even make a road in the wilderness
and rivers in the desert.

Allow the Lord to deliver you and allow Him to keep you. He will make a way for your deliverance. You have to want it and desire to maintain it as well.

When the Lord delivers you from that lifestyle of sin, the drugs/alcohol, unclean spirits, or soul-ties, keep the gift. Keep your vessel clean and filled with the things of God

Jesus desires for us to be set free, for we belong to Him.

Prayer

Lord Jesus, I have sinned against you. I repent of these sins: (list all sins)

Lord, please deliver me completely from any stronghold that Satan or his demons may have on me.

Please forgive me, Lord, and cleanse me from all unrighteousness. Strengthen me, Lord, by the power of your Holy Spirit.

I ask all these things in the precious name of Jesus.

*Continue to pray to Him.
Worship Him as your Deliverer and
Always keep His Word.*

Remember that He loves you and He desires to set every captive free.

CHAPTER 12

Question 12:
How Can I Become Closer
To God?

INTIMATE WITH GOD

One teenager asked me, how could I be close with God? I answered, "By being intimate with Him." *Revelation 3:20 says,*

"Behold, I stand at the door and knock.
If anyone hears My voice and opens the door,
I will come in to him and dine with him, and he with Me."

The Lord desires an intimate relationship with His children. *"... I will come in to him and dine with him, and he with Me."* The Lord is a true gentleman. He doesn't force Himself on anyone. He desires our loyalty, trust, love, praise, faithfulness, obedience, and intimacy.

Intimate is defined by The American Heritage dictionary as:

1. close acquaintance, association, or familiarity
2. essential; innermost.
3. comfortably private
4. very personal a close friend or confidant

This is what the Lord wants, intimacy with His people. How can one become intimate with Jesus? It's simple. Think of a relationship you have formed with a good friend. The friendship began when you were first introduced; therefore, the two of you became *acquaintances.*

Through conversations and perhaps activities you began to learn more about that person such as their ways, moods, attitudes, and personality. You became *friends* the more time you spent with each other. And with time, you may have developed feelings for that person as you began to *trust* that person. A relationship developed. Needs were met. You now have a friend, a companion, a confidant. *Intimacy* begins when you start to share your innermost thoughts with your friend. You took that friend to a personal level allowing them to know private things about you. Why wouldn't you? You two are intimate.

Reflection

A Story of Intimacy

Years ago I met a very romantic and sensitive man named Calvin Jamison, a.k.a. C.J. C.J. had a beautiful spirit. This man taught me how to be appreciated, respected, and loved. The Lord sent this man my way to minister to me. C.J. spoke to the true princess in me.

C.J. was a soldier and because of his career, our court-ship was short lived. He was stationed on the other side of the country. There was a great deal of sadness associated with his leaving. Often I would ask the Lord why I met him, fell so hard for him and why he had to move away. I wanted a relationship with him, an intimate one.

Months after C.J. moved away, the Lord brought this man and our courtship back to my attention. I remembered why I was so infatuated with this man.

He was considerate and thoughtful. He would hold my hand in the movie theater and guide me up the steps through the darkness. I have awful nighttime vision and am at anyone's mercy walking in the dark. C.J. was so respectful. Even when the actress appeared on the screen looking lovely and radiant, he didn't whoop and holler like the rest of the men in the theater. He may have appreciated this woman's beauty as did I, but he respected me and

.... made sure I knew that I had his attention.

We would talk about our dreams, our plans and the future. One of my favorite memories about C.J. was when he would sing to me. The first time I met C.J. he was singing. He had a beautiful voice. He was always serenading me.

He was full of happiness and gladness.

He accepted my decision to be celibate. I told him about my decision to wait early in our relationship. In no way did I want to mislead him. His reactions let me know so much about this man. He gave me a beautiful compliment, "That is beautiful, you are special. I guess I need to bring you roses each time I see you because you are so special." That, if nothing else sealed the deal! He will forever be imprinted on my brain for that line only if nothing else. Yes, it could have been fake or phony but he said it. Most important, his actions toward me backed up his compliment.

Whenever we would go out to eat, C.J. would share his food with me and even feed it to me. He treated me like a "little sister" watching over me and respecting me.

One summer I was watching C.J. with his niece, a busy little three-year old. She, like myself craved C.J.'s attention. While C.J.'s brother was washing the car, the little girl dipped her hands in the dirty, soapy water and headed directly toward C.J. to wipe her hands on his clothes.

Now C.J., being extremely dapper, always dressed nice. She was about to mess up a very nice, expensive white, silk shirt. After some quick maneuvering on his part, he avoided her hands on his clothes but caught her hands in his hands. Her hands now in his, landed on the papers he was holding.

C.J. was so gentle with her. He never even raised his voice. He moved his body quickly to avoid her filthy little hands but was quick enough catch her hands in his hands thus allowing her to ruin his papers. Initially I thought, wow what a bad little girl. Then I thought, no she isn't bad. She was a good little girl but was trying to "be bad" to get this man's attention. She was like me.

There were plenty of times I wanted to act bad to get his attention. I, a good girl, one who served the Lord living a lifestyle of celibacy, was trying to act bad to get his attention. What a lesson I learned from watching this little girl. She had showed me, me!

Still trying to get attention, his niece climbed up on the jeep while her father was trying to move into reverse. Fearful that she might get hurt, her dad asked C.J. to get her down. C.J. reached for his niece, grabbed her little wrist, allowed her to step out of the jeep, waited for her to get her feet on the ground, pulled her gently but firmly toward his side, looked up at the moving jeep to make sure she was out of harm's way and then looked down at her to make sure she was okay.

In the 15 seconds that it took for all of this to happen, my body nearly collapsed on the pavement. I couldn't believe what I'd just witnessed. His gentle actions made my knees buckle beneath me and I had to catch myself. C.J. was doing something that God does daily for us. He pulls us out of harm's way, gently. Even when we make bad decisions trying to fulfill our own will, Jesus is always with us. He knows what's best for us and He desires that we aren't harmed or hindered in any way. He even shows us the danger signs or may send someone our way to shout, "Get Down," or "Get Out of There," or even, *"Let it Go!"*

Not heeding the Lord's warnings, "we" tend to stay in our messes for so long that we can't make it down or make it out on our own. So the Lord steps in, lifts us up, turns us around, places our feet on solid ground. He delivers us. He pulls us near out of the way of danger, out of the direction of the enemy, the storm, the battle, and brings us closer to Him. Then He looks at us to make sure that we are okay. In other words, He looks at us to see what our other needs are. Jesus is a Great Deliverer and an Intimate Friend!

This is why I nearly fell to the pavement. I was witnessing a man in the flesh but seeing a much bigger picture! I was watching the characteristics of God! There is truly no comparison between man and God. For the sake of explaining intimacy, however, I have compared a few things from our relationship. I write this reflection story to show you what the Lord allowed me to see. I needed to fall in love with Him like I had fallen for C.J. I was courting with a man and at the same time trying to court God. It didn't work. We can't serve God and mammon (*Matthew 6:24*).

I became so distracted when this man stepped into my life; I was just as bad as one of those teenage boys who whooped and hollered at the movies. The Lord played back my intimate relationship with C.J. to show me what I should do with Him. The Lord showed me that I needed to step into a secret, quiet place with Him and sing songs to Him. I needed to learn the character of Jesus and become familiar with His ways, His presence, and His voice. I needed to continue to seek the face of God. I needed to spend quality time with Him. I needed to acknowledge Him at all times, at home, in the car, on the job, at school, and in my free time. I needed to share my thoughts, my dreams, my plans, my future, and my meals with the Lord. I needed to humble myself and ask God for His will, then obey! I needed to be able to say, "Your Will, Lord, not mine," and mean it.

Meeting C.J. was an eye-opener for me. After the courtship ended, I couldn't help but think of the man I would someday marry.

Steps toward intimacy:

1) Salvation is the start.

As followers of Christ, it is essential for you to know Him, believe Him, and trust Him. When *"...you confess with your mouth the Lord Jesus and believe in your heart that God raised Him from the dead, you will be saved" (Romans10: 9).*

As a follower, it's important to take the proper steps toward salvation. This is necessary for forming a relationship with Jesus.

2) Repent of all of your sins. Learn to die to your flesh and live in God *(Romans 6:11)*. *"..Reckon yourselves to be dead indeed to sin, but alive to God in Christ Jesus our Lord. Therefore do not let sin reign in your mortal body, that you should obey it in its lusts."*

Sin separates us from the Lord. Humbleness, brokenness, and willingness bring us closer to Jesus. Paul discussed how he had to die to sin on a daily basis *(1 Corinthians 15:31).*

3) Worship Him for Who He is. Sing praises to Him. Read the scriptures out loud to allow the Word of God to move in your Spirit, out of your mouth directly to the ears of your Heavenly Father.

Why Intimacy?

1) *"Oh, taste and see that the Lord is good; blessed is the man who trusts in Him!" Psalms 34:8*

This may be a hard step for some of us. Learning how to trust the Lord with our lives requires us to be obedient to His will. We aren't normally obedient to anyone we don't yet trust. And we can't trust those that we don't know. So know Him, taste and see that the Lord is good. Ask for guidance, listen and obey His word. Ask the Lord to lead you throughout the day so that you may please Him in all of your ways. Ask the Lord to bless you so that you may glorify Him.

2) Know Him and know His ways.

> *"...show me now Your way, that I may know*
> *You and that I may find grace in Your sight..."*
> *Exodus 33:13*

You can rest assured that Jesus knows everything about you.

> *"Before I formed you in the womb I knew you;*
> *Before you were born I sanctified you; ..."*
> *Jeremiah 1:5*

He knows your sitting down and rising up. He understands your thoughts afar off *(Psalm 139)*. The Lord desires for us to know Him, believe Him, and understand Him.

181

Isaiah 43:10
"You are My witnesses, says the Lord,
And My servant whom I have chosen,
That you may know and believe Me,
And understand that I am He."

3) *Draw near to God and He will draw near to you*
(James 4:10).

You draw near to God by studying His word, seeking Him in prayer, and having an everyday conversation with your Father. Seek Him with your whole heart!

Jeremiah 29:11-13
"For I know the thoughts that I think toward you, says the Lord, thoughts of peace and not of evil,
to give you a future and a hope.
Then you will call upon Me and go and pray to me,
and I will listen to you.
And you will seek Me and find Me, when you search
for Me with all your heart."

Reading the Word of God will bring you into a closer relationship. You will learn more about the Lord through His Word.

I Peter 2:2 "desire the pure milk of the word, that you may grow thereby, if indeed you have tasted that the Lord is gracious." This milk that Peter refers to is the best nourishment for our growth as Christians. Study the scriptures, meditate on the word, and believe.

4) Humbly sit at His feet. Set an atmosphere to praise, worship, and listen to the Lord. By sitting at His feet, you are putting all other things to the side so that you can devote quality time

with Jesus. Spending time with Jesus is a great opportunity to sing praises to Him, listen to Him and talk with Him.

Devotional time shows the Lord that you are willing to listen to Him, care about the concerns of Jesus, and it shows your availability and willingness. Go into a secret place with Jesus like your bedroom so that you can worship on you own in your own way. Put your entire daily cares aside and worship, talk to Jesus, and meditate on His word.

> *"Your word, I have hidden in my heart,*
> *That I might not sin against You.*
> *Psalm 119: 11*

> *Psalm 119:33*
> *Teach me, O Lord, the way of Your statutes,*
> *And I shall keep it to the end.*

5) Know that you are loved perfectly.

> *"Greater love has no one than this, than to lay down one's*
> *life for his friends."*
> *John 15:13*

The Lord loves you. He gave Himself for you to give you every opportunity, to cleanse you and to present you as holy (*Ephesians 5:25-29*).

The Result of Intimacy

> *The more intimate you are with the Father, the more*
> *Christ-like you become!*

The more time you spend with Jesus, the more you become like Jesus. You will eventually think like Him, care about the things He cares about, and become compassionate like Him because we tend to become like those we are around often.

Have you ever seen married couples that tend to talk alike, say the same things, and think alike? Some of them even look alike! Intimate partners tend to become reflections of one another. As intimate partners with Jesus, we will become a reflection of Him to the point where people will know you are a follower of Jesus.

My friend Arky explained how spending time with Christ would become evident to others by reminding me of Peter. Peter denied knowing Jesus; however, it was indeed obvious to the townspeople that Peter was with Jesus. The reflection of the Spirit of God was all over Peter.

Mark 14:67
And when she saw Peter warming himself, she looked at
him and said,
"You also were with Jesus of Nazareth."

Peter denied it.

Mark 14:69
And the servant girl saw him again, and began to say to
those who stood by,
"This is one of them."

Peter denied it again.
The girl went on to say,

" ...Surely you are one of them; for you are a Galilean,
and your speech shows it."
Mark 14:70

Peter denied it the third time and ran away from the people who accused him. Peter couldn't escape the presence of the Spirit of God, however. The Holy Spirit was all over Peter because he and Jesus had been intimate.

Consider Moses. After returning from the mountaintop where he fellowshipped with God, he had to wear a veil because the glory of God was shining upon him so radiantly.

II Corinthians 3:18
"But we all, with unveiled face, beholding as in a mirror the glory of the Lord, are being transformed into the same image from glory to glory, just as by the Spirit of the Lord."

Other Results & Benefits

Intimacy with Christ brings about a change in you. Intimacy causes you to stand out from the others, stand out from the rest of the world, and become radiant, holy, and pure in mind, thoughts and action. Submitting your will becomes easier, your burdens become lighter, your faith is simpler, and you easily trust God because you know your Husband, your Heavenly Father, has it all under control!

God longs to be with His people in spirit/worship. Be yoked with God! Be yoked to Him first! Your desires should be to please God and honor Him. We are His people. We belong to God. As a Christian, your life is to be different from those in the world. You must learn to have an intimate relationship with the Lord before you have one with another. You learn the correct way to balance your love and commitment once you are connected to the Lord.

When you love the Lord "first" you will know Him and be able to obey Him. You will be able to love others, as the Lord will have you to love them.

" ...as I have loved you, that you also love one another"
John 13:34

Through the relationship I had with C.J., I learned intimacy. The Lord also showed me what He desired from His people, intimacy. The Lord desires our worship, faithfulness, devotion and loyalty, availability, willingness, and commitment. Everything we ask for in a man, God is! The Lord is a loyal, true, and faithful friend. He desires us to be the same type of friend. I've learned a new way of living. I am living to honor my Father, my Husband, the lover of my soul.

Jesus woke me with an answer to prayer. He never fails me (*I Corinthians 13:8*).

He answers all prayers. One day I realized my past mistakes with men. I quietly told the Lord my new revelation. "Each man I was dating was a distraction from You, Lord. I'm sorry I allowed myself to be so distracted. If You just send someone my way that loves You like I love You than there would be no problem. So I need a man with the Holy Spirit, a man on fire for You. I need a man who loves You and is willing to submit to You. I need a man who's truly committed to You. I need that type of man." I then thanked the Lord for the revelation and continued about my day.

The Lord answered my prayer. It's important to always put God first.

Intimacy with Christ causes you to become yoked together, bound or knitted together and one with Him. His desires will be your desires, and He is there with you always. The Lord desires an intimate relationship with all of us because after all we are His people, His bride.

Bridal Path
A glorious opportunity!

The Lord has chosen us, the children of God to be His bride, the Church. He desires for us to be dressed in white linen and present ourselves without blemishes, stains, nor wrinkles (*Ephesians 5:27*).

Our job is to be prepared and ready for the Bridegroom. Imagine a wedding ceremony, the bride fussing about trying to make the right preparations. She is excited and ready to meet her destiny. So, can you imagine a bride running around on her special day in search of a much-needed item? Of course not, she would have everything in advance. She should be ready!

Remember the ten virgins who traveled to meet the Bridegroom? Some of the virgins were wise and brought along extra oil for their lanterns. They were spiritually prepared. The other virgins were not as wise. They were foolish not to bring their extra oil. They were simply not prepared. They asked the wise virgins for some of their oil. These prepared ladies knew they couldn't share their oil because they would then run out. The unprepared virgins decided to venture out to find more oil. While out trying to find oil, the Bridegroom came and opened the door for the virgins who were ready. When the unprepared virgins returned, the door was closed to them.

They cried out, *"Lord, Lord open to us!" (Matthew 25:11)*.

The Lord answered saying, *"...I do not know you" (Matthew 25:12)*.

The foolish virgins were ill prepared and as a result of that, they missed a glorious opportunity.

Jeremiah 2:32
"Can a virgin forget her ornaments,
Or a bride her attire?
Yet My people have forgotten Me days without number."

Don't let the cares of this world distract you from the things of God. Be prepared to share an intimate moment with God. You don't want to miss your blessing! Take for an example the story of Martha and her sister Mary.

In *Luke 10:38-42*, Martha welcomed Jesus into her home. She then busied herself with housework. Her sister, Mary, however, sat at Jesus' feet, listening to Him. Martha then approached Jesus saying, *"Lord, do You not care that my sister has left me to serve alone? Therefore tell her to help me"* (*Luke 10:40*).

Jesus answered her saying,

"Martha, Martha, you are worried and trouble about many things. But one thing is needed, and Mary has chosen that good part, which will not be taken away from her."
Luke 10:41-42

How many of us are like Mary running to sit at the feet of Jesus and fellowship with Him? How many of us are like Martha, busying ourselves with the cares of the world? Often I wonder what Martha was doing exactly to miss out on a grand opportunity such as fellowshipping with Jesus. Then I realized she was doing what we all have been guilty of doing. We allow the world to distract us and we don't give ourselves the opportunity to sit at the feet of Jesus and have devotion.

With intimacy comes commitment

Commitment

The Lord woke me one morning and dropped in my spirit the words "bridal path." I laughed. To me this was funny, because I'd been asking the Lord for confirmation regarding marriage. He answered me several times and in several ways; however, I wanted to be sure. Perhaps the Lord wanted to make sure I wasn't doubtful again and dropped this in my spirit, immediately waking me from sleep. I had been closer to the Lord than ever before. Months earlier I had made a decision to follow Jesus. I told the Lord that I wanted to be

His bride, His woman! I was so determined to pursue the things of God. Being so much in love with Jesus, I knew He was all that I wanted and all that I needed.

Intimacy is covering

Covered

The role of the wife is to take care of the needs of the Husband. The Lord told me years ago to take care of His house and He would take care of mine. His house could mean His children, or His generation, and even His vessel. The Lord wanted me to continue my work with His generation. My burden is for young people, especially young women. I believe He also wanted me to protect His dwelling place, my body.

The Lord definitely takes care of my house. He is my covering. Do you remember when Naomi told Ruth to sit at Boaz's feet? Ever wonder why? She knew that this was a way to show humility. She knew that Boaz would respect her for this humble act. Boaz desired to be Ruth's covering. Boaz desired to look after this young maiden, to protect her and her family.

A covering is a symbol of protection. It's something that conceals or shields. My Husband is the Lover of my soul, my Lord, my Covering, and my Love. We as followers of Jesus are covered, blood covered!

Psalm 17:8
"Keep me as the apple of Your eye; Hide me under the shadow of Your wings,.."

Psalm 57:1
Be merciful to me, O God, be merciful to me!
For my soul trusts in You;

189

And in the shadow of Your wings I will make my refuge

Intimacy with your Heavenly Father is a vital step in remaining celibate until marriage. Desire intimacy with Him and maintain that relationship! You are the bride and He is the Bridegroom. Allow this level of intimacy to keep you holy for He is holy. You have a Friend, a Husband, a Covering and a Great Lover of your soul forever.

Revelation 19:7-8
"Let us be glad and rejoice and give Him glory,
for the marriage of the Lamb has come, and His wife has
made herself ready. And to her it was granted to be arrayed
in fine linen, clean and bright, for the fine linen is
the righteous acts of the saints."

Prayer for intimacy

Oh Lord, how I desire to be close to You.

Allow me to hear Your voice.

Help me to do Your will and Your way.

Give me peace, leadership, and guidance as I follow after You.

I want to sing praises to You and worship You.

I want to give You my full attention.

I want to please You in all of my ways.

PART IV

How Can I Turn My Life Around?

CHAPTER 13

Question 13: Is Being Celibate Difficult?

It's All a Faith walk

Many have asked, "Is being celibate difficult? My answer is "absolutely, but its possible!"

A boat carrying the disciples was being tossed in a storm on the sea. Jesus walked on water toward the disciples and spoke to the men to calm their anxiety and fear.

Jesus said,

"...Be of good cheer! It is I; do not be afraid.
And Peter answered Him and said,
Lord, if it is You,
command me to come to You on the water,"

So He said, "Come."

*And when Peter had come down out of the boat, he walked
on the water to go to Jesus.
But when he saw that the wind was boisterous,
he was afraid; and beginning to sink he cried out, saying
Lord, save me!
And immediately Jesus stretched out His hand and caught
him, and said to him,*

"O you of little faith, why did you doubt?"

Matthew 14:27-31

In case you are wondering what a faith walk is exactly,
know that it is what you are doing right now as you read
this book. As you read, you are taking a bold step into a new
lifestyle of celibacy. You are stepping into a lifestyle that
may be brand new to you, a lifestyle that is unfamiliar, a lifestyle that follows the direction of God. Living a lifestyle of
celibacy means that you no longer will walk in the familiar,
having intimate relationships with men, but you will now
create an intimate relationship with the Lord.

A faith walk is a submission of your will, boldly stepping
out on faith, and believing God for your future. Making the
decision to remain celibate until marriage is a difficult decision. Along your journey you will be tempted, pressured,
and you will doubt your very own actions. This chapter was
written to simply encourage your heart, motivate your spirit,
and demonstrate that all things are possible.

My life is a faith walk because whatever the Lord desires
me to do, I will. Whatever paths He wants me to take, I will.
I'm stepping into my destiny, trusting, and depending on my
trusted Leader and Guide, Jesus!

Without intimacy, it's hard to stay in the faith walk. A
biblical example of an intimate relationship tried in faith is
God and Abraham. They were intimate friends (II *Chronicles
20:7*). Abraham and God talked like you and I would face

to face. They made covenants (promises) to one another. One night Abraham asked God for a child because he was concerned that he would not have an heir. God answered his friend who was then called Abram.

Genesis 15:5-6
Then He brought him outside and said, "Look now toward heaven, and count the stars if you are able
to number them."
And He said to him, " So shall your descendants be."
And he believed in the Lord, and He accounted it to him for righteousness.

God later blessed Abraham and his wife Sarah with a son named Isaac even though Abraham and Sarah were very old. Then God did the unthinkable. He tested Abraham, asking him to sacrifice his beloved son, Isaac.

Genesis 22:1
Now it came to pass after these things that God tested Abraham, and said to him, "Abraham!" And he said,
"Here I am."
Then He said, "Take now your son, your only son Isaac, whom you love, and go to the land of Moriah, and offer him there as a burnt offering on one of the mountains of which I shall tell you."

Abraham set out in the morning with firewood, two servants, a donkey, and his son. He went to the place that God had instructed. Along the trip, Isaac asks his father where the offering was.

Genesis 22:8-12
And Abraham said, "My son, God will provide for Himself
the lamb for a burnt offering."

So the two of them went together.
Then they came to the place of which God had told him.
And Abraham built an altar there and placed the wood
in order; and he bound Isaac his son and laid him on the
altar, upon the wood.

And Abraham stretched out his hand and took the knife to
slay his son.
But the Angel of the Lord called to him from heaven and
said, "Abraham, Abraham!" So he said, "Here I am."
And He said,
"Do not lay your hand on the lad, or do anything to him;
for now I know that you fear God, since you have not with-
held your son, your only son, from Me."

Abraham then lifts his eyes and finds a ram behind him
trapped in a bush. Abraham took the ram offered it as an
offering instead of his son.

Genesis 22:14-18
And Abraham called the name of the place, The-Lord-Will
Provide; as it is said to this day, "In the Mount of the Lord
it shall be provided."
Then the Angel of the Lord called to Abraham a second
time out of heaven, and said; By Myself I have sworn, says
the Lord, because you have done this thing and have not
withheld your son, your only son—

"Blessing I will bless you, and multiplying I will multiply
your descendents as the stars of the heaven and as the

sand which is on the seashore; and your descendants shall
possess the gate of their enemies.
In your seed all the nations
of the earth shall be blessed, because
you have obeyed My voice."

Reflection story

Stepping out on faith is difficult. Following the Lord's instructions and directions is especially difficult when you can't see where He is leading you. But that's what faith is. Believing and trusting in things we can't see! Even now, as I write this book, I am standing on faith believing that the Lord has me just where I am for a divine purpose. It's difficult but I believe in the Lord's plans for my life.

I'm eager to trust God because I have no reason to doubt Him. He is real and very present in my life. The Lord is a promise keeper! I just have to continue to write my visions and keep my eyes on the prize even if I can't physically see the intended goal.

Years ago, I went rock climbing with a group of friends from college. Being an experienced climber, I decided to try a difficult climb called "Jacob's Ladder." This rock was nearly straight up in the air. Halfway up on my first attempt to climb this rock, I lost my grip and was falling.

Not only was I falling but also swinging down with great speed because I had climbed an "easier" route on the left side of the rock. Being an experienced climber, I felt confidant and figured that my belay man had control of my fall. The belay man is the brakeman. The belay man secures the climber at the end of the rope. If a climber is in danger, the belay man can pull the slack and catch or break a climber before they fall completely. Because I had taken an "easier" route, I had put myself into a situation in which I could not have been caught or stopped by the brakeman. With seven people watching in fear, I was headed for a nasty crash down.

One of the guides dove for me in an attempt to break my fall. Now I wasn't hurt physically. Neither was the guide. My pride however was a bit damaged, and I decided to give it another shot to save face. My legs shook horribly beneath me. Every muscle in my arm burned and ached from the previous attempt. I tried four or five times to get back up but couldn't. I was mentally and physically drained. I told the girls who were cheering me on; that I was giving it up for I was truly tired. They understood.

Some time later, one of the girls in our group made it to the top of that difficult climb. I was impressed and thought about trying the rock again. Something else, however, was claiming my attention. It wasn't necessarily a big challenge like Jacob's Ladder but it was a "faith walk" to some extent. The rock was called "Granny's Norge" and it appeared to be a simple route. As a matter of fact, I climbed that route and repelled down that same hill a day before. The only difference with this particular climb was that each climber would climb blindfolded!

"I press toward the mark, forgetting those things that are behind" (Phil 3:13-14).

I thought to myself "Why not, I will try." With my trusted new friend and belay man, Rose, I put on my gear, chalk bag, carabineers, attached myself to Rose and lastly tied the blind-fold around my head, covering my eyes.

Without vision for the first time ever in climbing, fear set in. Thinking about the earlier climb and fall, I almost called it quits before I even started. Yet, I was up for the challenge. Once I started up the rock, I felt uneasy. I remember saying a prayer. I remember reaching for finger holds and wondering if I was going up a smooth route or rough route. In rock climbing, you want to climb in areas where there are plenty of crevices and holes in order to help stabilize yourself while climbing. I felt around slowly and then sporadically at times trying to find a good place to grab. I was doing it. I was climbing without vision! None!

All of my senses were working overtime. I was so close to the rock with my entire body. With my face so close to the mountainside, I could actually smell and taste the wet rock beneath me. I could hear the girls down below yelling for me to keep moving. The encouragement was great until one point when I heard someone say, "Uh Oh!" I thought who would say that, Uh Oh? Am I in trouble? Is she watching me or another climber?

After making it to the top, I removed the blindfold and repelled down successfully.

After touching ground, I realize why the girls got quiet and why someone blurted, "Uh Oh!" It appears that I was headed for a smooth route, one with little to no hand- holds, crevices or obvious bumps. It's ironic because the hardest part was the part I breezed through with ease. Perhaps I breezed through the rough part because I didn't see it. I was totally blind to the fact that I was in a dangerous territory. Even laying flat on the smooth places, I didn't panic. I knew I would have to work hard to find a handhold and I did. If I had seen this dangerous route, I would have definitely avoided it.

This day I truly amazed myself! This experience caused me to reflect on myself, my self-esteem, and my faith in self and in God.

I can't take all of the credit because I know I had a trustworthy belay man underneath me, Rose. Each step I made I could feel my rope become snug because she was working her little arms to keep up with me. Rose would pull in the slack and kept her eyes on me. When I moved she moved. When I rested upon the rock, she would keep her hands to her side locking me into position, which is what we, call "breaking."

God is our Belay Man! God keeps us secure in our "faith walk." The Lord is always watching us, our every move. God is my trustworthy belay man. The Lord wants us to continue our faith walks, our faith climbs, until we make it! You have got to depend on Him. He has got it all under control.

You can't trust just anyone with your rope. You just can't give your rope to anyone. The same goes for your heart and your life. I look at my lifestyle of celibacy as a faith walk, trusting and depending on the Lord for all of life's successes. My day of climbing allowed me the opportunity to experience failure and it allowed for me to experience success. I may have fallen once or twice, but I reached inside for the strength to *"keep on moving!"*

With the encouragement from others and the support of an Anchor, which in my case was the belay man, anything was possible. I am anchored in by the grace of God. My rope is like an umbilical cord tied into my Mother, Father, Protector, and Provider. A climber and their belay man are one! They are a team. I am so glad to be one with Jesus. We are a great team. When I am doubtful, He is the Word, the Truth, the Light and the Way.

James 1:2-6
"My brethren, count it all joy when you fall into various
trials, knowing that the testing of your faith
produces patience.
But let patience have its perfect work, that you may be
perfect and complete, lacking nothing.
If any of you lacks wisdom, let him ask of God,
who gives to all liberally and without reproach,
and it will be given to him.

But let him ask in faith, with no doubting, for he who
doubts is like a wave of the sea driven and
tossed by the wind."

In our faith walks, we must remember to count it all joy. The Lord is not finished with us yet. There may still be places in your life that the Lord needs to make whole, complete. Be encouraged. Keep on moving! Never stop your progression, just keep on climbing, and keep on pushing.

Please stay away from the naysayers, the ones who say negative things such as "you just failed, you will never make it or even "Uh Oh!" These people can discourage you and hinder your walk with Christ. Don't give anyone the opportunity to stop your progress. Faith is what moves God. We please God with our faith.

Psalm 18:35-36
"You have also given me the shield of Your salvation;
Your right hand has held me up,
Your gentleness has made me great.
You enlarged my path under me,
So my feet did not slip."

Sister in Christ, I believe!

Poem
Doubt sees the obstacles,
Faith sees the way
Doubt sees the darkest night,
Faith sees the day
Doubt dreads to take a step,
Faith soars on high,
Doubt questions, "Who believes?"
Faith answers, "I."

Author unknown

CHAPTER 14

Question 14:
Do I Make A Verbal Commitment To Family And Friends Or Just To God?

I PROMISE

James 5:12
But let your "Yes" be "Yes;" and your "No", No," lest you fall into judgment.

"I promise" is about making a commitment to the Lord. When you make a promise you set yourself apart from the others. When you make a promise, you make a vow. You are making a commitment, a promise, or a vow to your Spiritual Husband.

Living a lifestyle of celibacy is the intention of waiting to be promised to your husband. You are making a decision to keep yourself and be "kept" for marriage. Writing down your goals and making them known is a vow, a promise to keep yourself faithful, holy, and consistent in all your ways. Once the promise is made or the vow taken, then your behavior and your actions should change to match your new title as a woman of God.

I took a vow years ago to remain celibate. I used to buy a new diary each year in December to start in January. I would write down goals on the hard cover of each journal. Each year I would write, "remain a virgin until marriage." It's not entirely clear how this goal got started. Perhaps I was holding onto a dream of marrying a wonderful man who loved God, a man who would treat me like a princess, a man who could appreciate his wife waiting for him. My mother always told me that and I believe the Lord taught me to match my desires with His desires.

Living a lifestyle of celibacy, we are expressing our dedication by refusing to have sex before marriage, avoiding intimate relationships with men and worshipping the Lord in our waiting. The Lord desires us to live a holy, sanctified life that is separated from worldly influences, avoiding corrupting influences, and avoiding sinful activities.

Living a lifestyle of celibacy means that we have separated ourselves from others to do a work for the Lord. We are promising to glorify the Lord with our walk and our talk. We vow to glorify the Lord with our bodies, duties, and service. A vow or promise is an obligation that binds. A vow is a way to dedicate oneself to God.

The American Heritage Dictionary defines the word vow as an earnest promise that binds one to a specified act or mode of behavior.

He was to be separated for the purpose of the Father. Taking a vow or making a promise is a serious event. Making a promise to the Lord should not be taken lightly. The Bible even warns us about making false promises.

Matthew 5:37
Jesus said, "Let your Yes be Yes and your No be No"

Proverbs 20:25
"It is a snare for a man...to reconsider his vows."

Do you believe what He has said? Can He believe in you? Can He trust your promises? Make your promise and take the vows just like a bride would with her bridegroom. Be wedded to the Father and take on the purpose of serving Him with your very life. Whatever the will of God is for your life, make a conscious decision to stay on course and be on purpose.

I promise

I am a child of God, a princess, a letter well written
(an epistle),
a witness, salt of the earth.
As a follower of Christ, a Christian, I realize that I represent the Church, which is known as the Bride of the Lamb, I am proud of the title, Bride; I will conduct myself to bring glory and honor to the Father, Son, and Holy Spirit regardless of what situation in which I find myself.
I will not allow my status as a child of God to treat others disrespectfully nor will I do anything less than be compassionate, loving, and kind as Jesus did.
Faithfulness, Commitment, and Loyalty are my responsibilities. For being faithful, committed and loyal is how I will honor and glorify the Father.
I will strive to remain holy, chaste, and pure.
I am aware of my role as a child of God. I will fulfill my responsibilities inherent in that role. All Christians are entitled to outstanding leadership, loyalty, and faithfulness.
I will provide that leadership.

I will be willing to walk in the path of the Lord my Savior.
I will openly state my beliefs, and will not put myself in a
position of compromise.
I will maintain a Christ-like character for I know
I am responsible for my actions. I will repent for my
wrongdoings.
I will seek the Lord's help for deliverance, healing, a
nd restoration.
I will earn the respect of my peers and those I witness to.
I will not compromise my integrity nor my moral standards
and beliefs.
I will not forget my name and who I represent, Jesus.
I am a Christian, a child of God, a princess, and I represent
the Kingdom of God.
I will glorify and honor the Lord as His Bride.
These things I promise in Jesus' Name.

CHAPTER 15

Question 15:
In This Day And Time, Do You Think I Can Make It?

Be Encouraged
Be Eager to Stand

Each person that I meet who knows of my personal testimony will ask this question, "How did you do it, why didn't you go all the way?" My answers vary but I generally go back to the foundation, which is the Word of God. If it weren't for the Word of God, I wouldn't be giving this testimony. I was not only convicted by the Holy Spirit but also moved by the strength and the love of God. I was determined to make it. I simply didn't want to give some man the opportunity to say that he "got me." I also never wanted to become pregnant before marriage because I knew it would hurt my family. I never wanted to have my name passed around by the boys in the locker room or by the boys my brothers played ball with. I wanted to share intimate moments with my husband ensuring that no man could run off after taking my treasure. This journey has not been easy. The days that I needed the Lord the most were the days that followed a breakup or when I was rejected because of my decision to wait.

When I felt intense pressure to have sex, I prayed. When I felt the stings of rejection, I got angry and wanted to get even by having the best man in marriage. I wouldn't dare give in to a man who put pressure on me. They didn't deserve me. But there were times when I was dating someone who I really enjoyed and really wanted to be with sexually. I needed strength and I needed a reason to keep my promise. Again, I prayed.

I recognize my dilemma as a battle of the flesh versus the spirit. I chose God over the sexual experience. I knew that He would never fail me and would provide more than I could ever imagine or want with that boyfriend.

I remember going through a spiritual battle years ago at work. My supervisor at the time wanted to fire me. Each day she would come in with some new problem for me to fix. After fixing the problems she would yell and humiliate me in front of the staff and clients. She made me so unhappy and the temptation to quit came with each day. After leaving work in tears, I was determined to find another job and quit. The next morning I woke up with great anxiety, knowing that I was to endure another challenging day. I drove to work and sat in my car with my Bible.

I read scriptures and tried to remember them verbatim. Then a story came to my remembrance. During the Great War, underage boys from Eton desired to fight in the war. These boys were eager; however, they had one major obstacle, their age. Because the enrollment officer of the British army had to ask the ages of the volunteers, the boys would write down the number 18 on a piece of paper and place it in their shoes. Therefore when asked their age, the boys wouldn't have to struggle with their answers, they were over 18!

I thought of the young Eton boys and figured I needed to stand on the Word of God so that no matter what happens throughout the day, I was still standing on the Word. I was physically standing on scriptures that I placed in my shoe. I was mentally focused on the scripture. I was living out the scriptures spiritually. I was eager to stand and not fall for anything my boss threw my way. Now I know this may sound ridiculous but I was at such a weak point, I wanted something to keep me focused on God's goodness. For me it worked. The Word of God was my mantra throughout the day. There were times when I focused more on my faith than on the roaring lion (the boss) that walked about trying to devour me. I was at peace.

Work became easier and I became less stressed. Eventually the Lord placed me in a new position. I relate this story to the one of celibacy because during your walk, you will come against many obstacles. Keep your mind on the promise, the Word of God. Allow the word to strengthen you and keep you in your time of temptation. Saying no to sexual activities will become easy and rejection from men will no longer stress you. You will be so focused on God's goodness that when men start coming your way trying to charm you, you will see right through it and be secure with your decision. Allow the Lord to move you in a position where you will find peace.

I hope this book has encouraged you to live a lifestyle worth celebrating. Each chapter is a reflection of what the Lord shared with me such as, reflections, personal stories of strengths, weaknesses, and lessons learned. Many young women who experienced sex prior to marriage have suffered from headaches and heartaches. If I could prevent every young woman from living an unsatisfactory lifestyle, I would. I pray this book will benefit you greatly. I want each young woman to enjoy her young life and celebrate each day with Jesus. That is my prayer!

Encouragement
Prayer

*Lord, I pray that I can learn how to celebrate a lifestyle
of celibacy.
Show me how much you love me Lord. Help me
to recognize who am I in You.*

*I pray that I discover the real treasures in my life. Remind
me that I am a true gem to you Lord. Give me a Christ like
character.*

*Help me to not rush or be anxious in dating. Help me to see
that your that your blessings will come.*

*Lord help me be aware of all traps and counterfeits on my
journey. I want to make good decisions in dating.*

*For all of those who have hurt me in the past, help me to
forgive. Show me how to repent and receive forgiveness.*

*I desire your deliverance from any (bondage, slavery,
soul-ties).*

Help me to develop an intimate relationship with You.

*I pray that I stay on Your desired path for your life and step
out in faith.*

*I want to be successful with my journey, keeping my
promise to you believing in Yours.*

I pray that you too will have a TESTIMONY to write and tell others about.

If you choose to wait you will be blessed. Remember these scriptures on your journey:

You can do all things through Christ who strengthens you (Phil 4:13).

Remember that God is able to do exceeding abundantly above all that we ask.
Ephesians 3:20

And know that there is nothing too hard for God!
Jeremiah 32:17

CHAPTER 16

How I Made It!

My Testimony

Often times a teenager or young adult will ask me how I made it. They want to know if my walk of celibacy is really possible. They are curious if one could really make it to the altar and be pure. I tell them that with Christ all things are possible.

One of my favorite biblical stories is the one of Abraham and Sarah. Sarah and Abraham were both old. Sarah wanted to bear a child for her husband; however, she was barren for many years. Due to her lack of faith she asked her hand-maiden to bear Abraham a child to produce an heir. After the birth of Ishmael, her handmaiden's child, Sarah became jealous and bitter. She thought her dreams of having a child were over.

Many years later, the Lord spoke to Abraham regarding the future son.

Why Laugh?

Genesis 18: 12, 14
Therefore Sarah laughed within herself, saying,
"After I have grown old, shall I have pleasure, my lord
being old also?"

And the Lord said to Abraham,
"Why did Sarah laugh, saying, Shall I surely bear a child,
since I am old?'

"Is anything too hard for the Lord?"

Isaac was in fact born in the time that the Lord appointed.
The name Isaac means Laughter.

Genesis 21:6
And Sarah said,
"God has made me laugh, and all who hear
will laugh with me."

After several years of trying to complete this book, I
desired to leave you with a closing testimony of how the
Lord blessed me for my faithfulness in Him. A few years
ago my pastor asked me about the book's completion and I
remember telling her that I was at a stand still. Pastor said
that I was to complete the book with a wedding.

A wedding? I laughed! I laughed like Sarah laughed. Not
because I didn't believe my pastor. The thought made me
happy but I truly couldn't see myself married by the end of
the year. Little did I know that I wouldn't finish the book
until a few years later, after my wedding.

The Message

A year before I married, the Lord gave me a message to share with women at a women's conference. The message was regarding a wedding scene. I decided that I would dress in white, have instrumental wedding music playing in the background and I would then parade down the aisle wearing a crown, holding my Bible. After reaching the pulpit I would turn to the audience and announce the wedding of the Church and the Bride Groom. It was to be very dramatic. I wanted people to feel as if they were witnessing a real wedding, having wedding programs and all. I was truly excited because the conference was in June, which is a popular month for weddings.

However, the month of June came and the Lord gave me a different audience to preach to and an entirely different message, "I Promise" for the young people. So after several months, I figured I would do the wedding message in the month of February, the "love" month and also use several scriptures from I Corinthians 13.

When February rolled around, I was sick with bronchitis. Unable to even attend church some days, I felt as if I lost my opportunity to preach the message. The Lord was setting me up for my very own wedding message! All the scriptures I wanted to use for my own sermon were actually used in my own wedding ceremony.

During that year, I was reading *God Chasers* for the second time and was really in hot pursuit of the Lord. I told the Lord that I wanted Him to be my Spiritual Husband and that I wanted to be His woman. The next day in Church, a guest Evangelist ministered to me. Two ministers at the service confirmed the Word that came from the Lord. One was ministry and the other was ministry in marriage.

For years, I knew I had a call on my life to minister. My burden has always been for young people. I was ready to work as an Evangelist. I had spoken at youth conferences numerous times and was now ready to serve God in any way possible. The second word ministry was for a marriage ministry. I didn't mention this to anyone. I didn't want people to try to fix me up with "brother so-and-so."

A month later after the ministry confirmation, I met my husband. The Lord began to give me confirmations regarding marriage with him. Personally, I felt I wasn't ready! I was so happy working as an Evangelist, learning scripture, attending classes and studying. I felt so filled with the Lord that I didn't want to make room for a boyfriend, let alone a husband. It wasn't long before I started to see what God had in store for me. My husband began to say things that only the Lord knew I needed to hear. The Lord loved me through this man and I couldn't deny it any longer. This was the man I was to marry.

After months of praying and fasting, the Lord began to show us our future. He answered our prayers!

Confirmations! He Answers Prayers

When my husband entered the picture I knew he was an answer to numerous prayers. He couldn't have been any better if I had written it out on paper. The Lord blessed me with my prince! When we became friends, I knew he was different, special. Soon the Lord would send confirmation from so many people regarding the marriage.

The Lord used the scripture I Corinthian 13:8 "Love never fails." This was a personal prayer that I used to write in my journal. Many years ago, I specifically asked the Lord to bless me with a good man because I was waiting for marriage. I had actually written in my journal that God was a Love that never failed! I knew His word would not return void. The Lord answered me with the same words and prayer I once written.

Believe it or not, after countless confirmations, I still wasn't convinced! Not because of my husband but because of the many changes that were to come about. My husband is in the military and I didn't want that lifestyle. It was hard imagining leaving family, career, and my business behind. At this particular time, I was also reading *The Prayer of Jabez* and was asking for the Lord to extend my borders/territory. The Lord did. He extended my location and knowledge beyond my wildest dreams.

In the beginning I was just so unsure if I was going in the right direction. So, the Lord woke me one morning and said "Bridal Path." This is the same thing He was showing me a year ago for ministry! Then I knew I was on the right path.

Confirmations! He Answers Prayers

After another word from the Lord at a church service, I called my fiancé up and told him that the Lord did answer us and that we were to pray for a wedding date. I was teaching at the time and needed to make sure I wasn't going to leave at a bad time during a school semester. My fiancé said that he already prayed and had a date. I said if we have the same date, then we know it's the date that the Lord selected for us. We all, Mitch, God and myself had February 16, in mind. That was our date. This would have never been our wedding date if left to us because we both despise cold weather and initially discussed having a summer wedding.

Message Delivered Finally!

The month of February came and everyone was predicting snow and ice. The Lord, however, gave us a glorious, beautiful 70-degree day! Yes, a warm sunny day in February. I couldn't have asked for a more beautiful day or wedding.

219

Decisions

The decision to make a vow of celibacy until marriage happened as a child. I used to buy a new diary each year in December to start in January. I would write down goals on the hard cover of each journal. Each year I would write, "remain a virgin." I don't even know how that all got started. I do believe God gave me that desire and I am still learning to match up His desires with mine. Learning the will of God is easy; however, living in His will is harder. We all battle with flesh and spirit. Don't put yourself in the midst of the storm constantly struggling. Know your strengths and weaknesses.

One day I realized my past mistakes with men. I quietly told the Lord my new revelation. "Each man I was dating was a distraction from You, Lord, and I am sorry I allowed myself to be so distracted. If you will send someone my way that loves You like I love You than there will be no problem. I know I need a man with the Holy Spirit. I need a man on fire for You. I need a man who loves You and one who is willing to submit to You. And I need a man that is truly committed to You. I need that type of man." Then I thanked the Lord for the revelation and continued about my day.

God blessed me with a saved husband, one who is on fire for God and one who treats me like a princess. I thank God for this opportunity to share my testimony with so many people. My life, my destination and my path are one of hope and success. I pray you will also find hope and great success on your journey. Take that bold step onto the path of righteousness. Remember God doesn't give us the spirit of fear but of power and of love and of a sound mind (*II Timothy 1:7*). You have that power inside you to make it. May God bless you in your decision to wait. May you find happiness and peace on your successful journey.

Prayer

I Peter 2:11

"Beloved, I beg you as sojourners and pilgrims, abstain from fleshly lusts which war against the soul, having your conduct honorable...."

I Thessalonians 4:1-4

"Finally then, brethren, we urge and exhort in the Lord Jesus that you should abound more and more, just as you received from us how you ought to walk and to please God; for you know what commandments we gave you through the Lord Jesus.

For this the will of God, your sanctification: that you should abstain from sexual immorality; that each of you should know how to possess his own vessel in sanctification and honor, not in passion of lust..."

RESOURCES

Bible scriptures were taken from The Holy Bible, New King James Version (Copyright © (1982) by Thomas Nelson Inc.

All definitions were taken from The American Heritage Dictionary of the English Language, 4th ed. Boston Houghton Mifflin, 2000.

About the author

F.S. Mitchell is a military spouse currently living in Europe where she speaks to youth and young adults about abstinence and spiritual living. Francis is a happily married NEWLYWED continuing living her life on purpose and as a promise.

For speaking engagements or other information contact F.S Mitchell at:

P.O Box 33
Prince George, VA 23875

Or go to www.fsmitchell.com or email her at celebrate@ fsmitchell.com

Printed in the United States
56849LVS00001B/220-345